My coursework planner

Section 1 Introduction

1.1 How to use this book

This book has been designed to help you to develop the skills necessary for success in your coursework for Edexcel A level History. The book is divided into four main sections to illustrate each stage of the process. Each section is made up of a series of topics organised into double-page spreads. On the left-hand page, you will find guidance on what is required to achieve the top grades, while on the right-hand page you will find activities that will help to inform your thinking and practice the skills required for a strong answer. (You may be familiar with this approach if you use the My Revision Notes A-level History revision guides.) Together, the guidance and activities will take you through the skills essential for coursework success.

It is important to have a clear strategy for your coursework. This workbook will help you to achieve this in a planned and logical way. Use this book as the cornerstone of your research and writing – it is designed to be written in so don't be afraid to make use of all the space to refine your ideas and thinking. The workbook will also come in handy when reflecting on your progress in discussion with your teacher.

Section 3 is made up of a number of activities that will help you prepare to analyse the **interpretations** you use in your coursework. The extracts* in this section have been taken from some of the more popular coursework topics, but don't skip over these to look for topics you are familiar with, as each activity has been designed to practise a different skill. The skills involved in summarising **arguments**, establishing **criteria** by which to judge interpretations and find their flaws, are universal and will help you regardless of the topic you have chosen for your coursework.

*Please note that for space, the extracts in this workbook are a lot shorter than the length expected in the coursework.

At the back of this book you will find several logs to record your progress. While the My Progress boxes throughout this workbook give you a chance to apply what you have learnt from an activity to your own coursework and to record some of your thinking, the logs at the back will serve as a working document that you should be adding to from day one.

You can find answers to some of the activities online at www.hoddereducation.co.uk/HistoryCoursework/Answers. These have the 'A' symbol to indicate this.

1.2 Key questions answered

What is the coursework about?

The coursework is worth 20 per cent of your A level grade. It focuses on interpretations, therefore you will need to analyse and **evaluate** the views of **three** chosen historians.

What can you write about?

The topic of the coursework must be one that has created a **debate** among historians. It can be narrow or broad in its timeframe but must have caused sufficient controversy for historians to have put forward a variety of views. There is one important restriction: you cannot write about the topic you have studied for the interpretations section of Paper 1 (Section C). You are permitted to write about a controversy related to other topics you have studied in Papers 1, 2 or 3, or write about an entirely new area of history. Section 2 of this book (pages 10–17) covers the considerations around choosing a topic and a title.

How much help can I get?

This is an independent study, so you cannot get specific help from your teacher on the writing of your essay. Your teacher is allowed to review one draft and indicate which elements of the assessment criteria are lacking but cannot give very detailed feedback. The way that the essay will be marked is explained on pages 7–9, however, the main thing to remember is that the research and the writing up *must be your own work*.

How long is the essay?

The essay should be 3000–4000 words in length. If you write fewer than 3000 words you would be unable to deal with the topic in sufficient depth. If you exceed 4000 words it is less likely that you will be able to produce a concise response, which is required for a high grade. The skills that you need to demonstrate can be shown effectively within the word length.

What kind of historical works can be used?

The three chosen works can be texts or audiovisual materials, but they must have been created by a recognised historian and be the product of appropriate research. Therefore, you should not use personal accounts or other primary sources, and you should not use history textbooks. In reality, the majority of suitable works you come across will be written academic texts. There is no requirement to read entire books and as a general rule your chosen works should be of article or chapter length (academic articles are usually around 7000 words in length).

The works do not have to have been produced recently. If, for example, you are writing about a medieval or early modern topic, it may be appropriate to use a Victorian account as long as it is a piece of academic history.

What sort of essay is required?

There are a number of key requirements for the essay.

- First, it is an 'essay' and requires continuous prose. There is no need for an elaborate or pretentious style, and the prose should be business-like and clear, but it must flow as a piece of writing. Recommended structures are discussed in Section 4 of this workbook, but you may choose to use subheadings to divide up the work.

- Though there are no specific marks for the quality of the English, to achieve a mark at Level 5 (33–40 marks), the argument should be logical and coherent. There is no objection to using a spell checker and you have plenty of time to check for typos and misspellings. A clear and readable font, such as Arial 12, is advisable. An appropriate referencing system, such as the use of **footnotes**, is expected when works are referred to and a **bibliography**, while not specifically marked, is required. Pages 68–69 will help you with this.

- This is an academic piece of work, so the wording of the title and the style should also be academic rather than journalistic in nature. The ideal level should be that of a good textbook with clear historical writing. Other models to follow might be sixth form historical magazines or history books accessible to sixth formers.

- Essays can describe events or offer a series of explanations, but this essay should focus on discussing and assessing the three historical interpretations. It should show your ability to make sustained and supported **judgements** on the interpretations, not just explain what happened in the past and why.

- In making these judgements, you should also use supplementary reading in the form of other texts by historians that are different to your chosen works. There is a requirement for at least two pieces of supplementary reading to be referred to but in order to access the higher bands in the mark scheme it would be sensible to use rather more than this.

What about schools of thought?

It is important not to get bogged down in **schools of history** (the collective beliefs of a number of historians who share similar points of view) as this can lead to simplistic and stereotypical **assumptions** being made about the work of an historian. For example, just because you know a historian is a Marxist does not necessarily mean their work will contain the same flaws as other Marxist historians. It is much more important that you focus on the *views* presented in the text itself.

Am I only writing about my three chosen works and nothing else?

In order to achieve a Level 5 response, it is important that you fully integrate **contextual knowledge** into your work. This means demonstrating sound knowledge and understanding of the debate and including relevant factual knowledge of the events you are discussing. It would be impossible to provide a full appraisal of the chosen works without this context.

What is the resource record and how does it work?

The resource record is a document that records all the reading you have done, whether it has been referenced in the main text or not. It helps to validate the assignment as your own work and it could prompt discussions with your teacher about your progress. In the 'comments' column you should provide evidence of why you have chosen your three works, including a short summary of the main differences between them.

What should be included when submitting the coursework?

- The essay itself, which must include a word count and a bibliography (normally ordered alphabetically by surname) of the works referred to in the text.
- The bibliography should distinguish between your three chosen works and extra reading.
- The resource record.
- A coursework authentication sheet, which must be signed by you.
- You are also allowed to submit an appendix with any extended extracts that help to put any quotations or sections of text you have referred to into context.

How is the essay marked?

The essay is initially marked by your teacher and if your school or college has a large number of students studying History, it may need to be moderated internally by another teacher. All schools and colleges then have to submit a sample to be assessed by an external **moderator** a month or so before your final exams.

1.3 The assessment criteria: demystifying the mark scheme

Assessment objective weighting

The assessment objective weighting for the coursework is as follows:

- AO1 – the ability to communicate knowledge and understanding, make substantiated judgements, explore concepts of cause, consequence, change, continuity, similarity, difference and significance – 25 per cent.
- AO3 – the ability to analyse and evaluate interpretations in relation to the historical context – 75 per cent.

To do well in your essay, it is important to understand the mark scheme. The ladders below contain the official wording of the mark scheme. To help you understand it, the text in the blue boxes provides a simplified version.

Level 1, 1–8 marks

- A limited range of material has been identified for use in the enquiry and appropriately cited. Information taken from reading is mainly used illustratively, and understanding of the issue in question is limited

This would typically refer to an answer that shows very little research has been carried out. Points made would be descriptive rather than analytical and the essay would ultimately fail to answer the question convincingly.

- Judgement on the question is assertive, with little or no supporting evidence, and contextual knowledge is not linked to it.

A judgement, or in other words a conclusion, about the answer to the question would be made but not backed up with evidence from the essay.

- Demonstrates only limited comprehension and **analysis** of the views in the three chosen works, selecting some material relevant to the question. Surface differences are noted as matters of information.

Comprehension refers to understanding something, so at this level there would be little understanding of the chosen works.

- Evaluation of the chosen works relates to their information rather than their **argument**, or is based on questionable assumptions.

Evaluation means 'giving value to', so an answer at this level would only decide how valuable the information (e.g. statistics put forward) from the chosen works is, rather than assessing the strength of the arguments.

- Some accurate and relevant knowledge is included but it lacks range and depth and does not directly address the enquiry. There are only limited attempts to structure the answer, and the answer overall lacks coherence and precision, but the work is concise.

Again, the answer would demonstrate that limited research has been carried out and would not be logically organised and structured.

Level 2, 9–16 marks

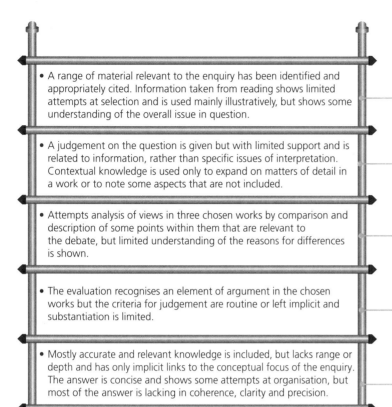

- A range of material relevant to the enquiry has been identified and appropriately cited. Information taken from reading shows limited attempts at selection and is used mainly illustratively, but shows some understanding of the overall issue in question.

- A judgement on the question is given but with limited support and is related to information, rather than specific issues of interpretation. Contextual knowledge is used only to expand on matters of detail in a work or to note some aspects that are not included.

- Attempts analysis of views in three chosen works by comparison and description of some points within them that are relevant to the debate, but limited understanding of the reasons for differences is shown.

- The evaluation recognises an element of argument in the chosen works but the criteria for judgement are routine or left implicit and substantiation is limited.

- Mostly accurate and relevant knowledge is included, but lacks range or depth and has only implicit links to the conceptual focus of the enquiry. The answer is concise and shows some attempts at organisation, but most of the answer is lacking in coherence, clarity and precision.

The knowledge displayed would be relevant but would only be used to make vague points, rather than to form convincing arguments.

Conclusions would not be backed up sufficiently, and would fail to take into account the strengths of the arguments in the chosen works.

At this level some basic differences between the chosen works would be pointed out but the answer would not get to the bottom of why these differences exist.

The answer would attempt to weigh up the strengths and weaknesses of the chosen works but would not make it clear on what grounds they have identified these.

The knowledge displayed would be appropriate but there would not be much of it. Like a Level 1 response, it would not be very well organised or structured and arguments would not always make sense.

Level 3, 17–24 marks

- A range of material relevant to the enquiry has been identified from reading and appropriately cited. Information has been appropriately selected and deployed to show understanding of the overall issue in question.

- A judgement on the question is related to some key points of view encountered in reading and discussion is attempted, albeit with limited substantiation. Contextual knowledge of some issues related to the debate is shown and linked to some of the points discussed.

- Analyses some of the views in three chosen works by selecting and explaining some key points and indicating differences. Explanation demonstrates some understanding of the reasons for differences.

- Attempts are made to establish valid criteria for evaluation of some arguments in the chosen works and to relate the overall judgement to them, although with weak substantiation.

- Mostly accurate and relevant knowledge is included to demonstrate some understanding of the conceptual focus of the enquiry, but material lacks range or depth. The answer is concise and shows some organisation. The general trend of the argument is clear, but parts of it lack logic, coherence and precision.

The answer would demonstrate a good level of research and this would be used to show the student has a sound grasp of the debate.

Conclusions would be made and these would come out of the points made in the essay, but would not be wholly convincing.

To analyse properly you need to carry out a detailed examination, and an answer at this level would start to do this with the chosen works but would not show a thorough understanding of why they have different views.

Criteria are a measure by which something can be judged. Valid criteria with which to measure the value of the chosen works will differ depending on the nature of the works, but what is vital is that the judgements you make are based on some kind of reasoning, rather than merely being asserted. An answer at this level would begin to do this but not in a convincing way.

Like a Level 2 response, the knowledge displayed would be appropriate but would be limited. Arguments would generally be clear and easy to follow but not always.

Level 4, 25–32 marks

- A range of material relevant to the enquiry has been identified from reading, appropriately cited and selected and deployed with precision to demonstrate understanding of the issues under debate. Most of the relevant aspects of the debate will be discussed, although treatment of some aspects may lack depth.

- Evidence from reading is used with discrimination to sustain a judgement on the question although selection may lack balance in places. Contextual knowledge of some of the issues is integrated in the discussion of aspects of the debate.

- Analyses the views in the chosen works and the differences between them, explaining the issues of interpretation raised. Explanation of points of view in three chosen works demonstrates some understanding of the basis of the arguments of the authors.

- Valid criteria are established by which the arguments in the three chosen works can be judged and they are applied in the process of making judgements, although some of the evaluations may be only partly substantiated.

- Knowledge is deployed to demonstrate understanding of the conceptual focus of the enquiry and to meet most of its demands. The answer is concise and generally well organised. The argument is logical and is communicated with clarity, although in a few places it may lack coherence and precision.

The answer would show a strong grasp of the debate but would not necessarily go into sufficient detail in some areas.

Like a Level 3 response, conclusions would be made and these would come out of points raised in the essay. Contextual information would be used to add weight and provide criticism of key arguments.

The views in the chosen works would be scrutinised convincingly and the answer would show a good understanding of why the authors have different views.

Conclusions about the strengths of the chosen works would be made and would relate to sensible criteria that the student has identified. What would fail to make this a Level 5 response would be a lack of full substantiation, i.e. plenty of evidence would be needed to back up the conclusions.

The answer would generally be convincing and would show understanding of the ideas associated with the debate. It would be well structured and most of the essay would be clear.

Level 5, 33–40 marks

- A range of material relevant to the enquiry has been identified from reading, appropriately cited and selected and deployed with precision to demonstrate understanding of the issues under debate. Most of the relevant aspects of the debate will be discussed in a sustained evaluative argument.

- Material from reading is used with discrimination to sustain a considered overall judgement on the question. Contextual knowledge of the issues is fully integrated into the discussion of the debate.

- Analyses the views in the chosen works and the differences between them, explaining the issues of interpretation raised. Explanation of points of view and differences between them demonstrates understanding of the basis of the arguments of the authors and the nature of historical debate.

- Valid criteria are established by which the arguments in the three chosen works can be judged and they are applied and fully justified in the process of making judgements.

- Knowledge is deployed to demonstrate understanding of the conceptual focus of the enquiry, and to respond fully to its demands. The answer is concise and well organised. The argument is logical and coherent throughout and is communicated with clarity and precision.

The knowledge deployed would all be sharply focused on the debate in the question. All the major arguments put forward would be fully assessed.

An overall judgement is reached based on a sophisticated understanding of all the reading, and well-integrated knowledge of the topic.

The arguments in the chosen works would be fully analysed and understood. Vitally for Level 5, there should be a full explanation of how and why the views differ.

The arguments in the three chosen works are judged, and the judgement is based on secure reasoning.

The answer would be succinct and there would be no irrelevant sections. There would be total focus on the issues in the question throughout and the argument would be very clear.

Section 2 Making a start

2.1 Choosing a topic

Your topic will either be given to you by your teacher or you will be given the opportunity to create your own question. If you are given a free choice, the information on this page will be useful to you.

When thinking about your topic, ideally, and in no particular order, consider the following.

- It might be something you have studied before but want to revisit in more depth.
- It might be something you studied previously that has grabbed your interest.
- It might be something you have read about and want to know more about.
- It might be something that affects your family or local area that you would enjoy researching.
- It might be the chance to look at the history of another continent – for example, Asia, South America or Africa.
- It might be something to show university admissions tutors that you are interested in different aspects of the subject and not afraid of tackling new topics.
- It might be that you really enjoy an established topic and would feel comfortable in extending your knowledge.

It should be able to deliver the requirements of the mark scheme.

- Most importantly, it should be a topic that has caused controversy or debate among historians.
- You should be able to find a range of interpretations to evaluate – i.e. there should be clear conflicting and contrasting views for you to weigh up to reach a judgement.
- It does not necessarily have to be a topic that has caused groundbreaking or bitter debates, but should at least contain different possible emphases and explanations that stress different factors.

It should be manageable.

- It should not be such a big topic that you cannot control the research and keep the essay to the 3000–4000 word limit.
- It should not require such detailed research that is more suitable for a PhD thesis. No one is expecting you to have to use a university library or incredibly specialised resources.
- It should be about something that you will understand. Sometimes complex topics sound good, but are just too demanding given the rest of your A level workload. It is generally better to produce a complex answer to a straightforward question than a simplistic answer on a complex topic.
- On the other hand, if you have an enquiring mind, don't opt for a topic that isn't going to offer enough challenge. Have confidence in your abilities, but be realistic.

Mind map

Below is an example of a mind map that a model student has made to map out their priorities in choosing a possible topic.

Order of importance:

1   I need stretch and challenge as I know I get bored easily and need to maintain interest in a long project.
2   Though it would be good to study Russian history, if I couldn't find debates I would be happy to look at another aspect of history, such as late-medieval England.
3   Though access to interpretations is important, I wouldn't mind venturing a little further than the school library to find them.

My progress

Now use the model above to set out your own priorities. Start by setting out which of the points in these three sections is most important.

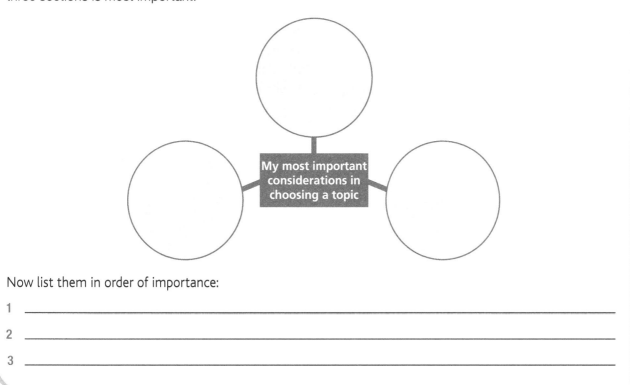

Now list them in order of importance:

1   _____

2   _____

3   _____

2.2 Choosing a title

Once you have settled on a topic or perhaps some suitable topics, the next task is to choose an appropriate title. All questions have to contain the following wording. All you will need to do is fill in the blanks.

Historians have disagreed about _____

_____ .

What is your view about _____

_____ ?

With reference to three chosen works:

- Analyse the ways in which interpretations of the question, problem or issue differ.
- Explain the differences you have identified.
- Evaluate the **arguments**, indicating which you found most persuasive and explain your judgements.

Is there a debate?

The question should lead to a debate and ultimately to a judgement about which historian's argument is most credible. If there is an obvious answer with little room for discussion, then the title won't work.

Are there enough interpretations?

There should be plenty of books and articles at an appropriate level for the topic and there should be the chance to look at more specialist studies. If it is a question that is particularly obscure, you might not be able to compile enough resources to answer the question sufficiently.

What kind of issues can the question cover?

There are a number of historical concepts that can be the subject of your question. They may include:

- Change, for example, 'What is your view about the impact of politics on changes to public health in the years 1750–1900?'
- Continuity, for example, 'What is your view about the reasons why Mussolini was able to maintain power in the years 1922–29?'
- Causation, for example, 'What is your view about how far religious differences were responsible for the outbreak of the English Civil War?'
- Consequence, for example, 'What is your view about the political consequences of the British policy of appeasement in the 1930s?'
- Similarity, for example, 'What is your view about how far Stalin's dictatorship was similar to Lenin's in the years 1928–1941?'
- Difference, for example, 'What is your view about why witch hunts in Scotland were more widespread than in England in the years 1580–1680?'
- Significance, for example, 'What is your view about the significance of Hitler to the maintenance of the Nazi dictatorship in the years 1933–1945?'
- Key features of a society or period, for example, 'What is your view about the experience of women in the Spanish Second Republic, 1931–1936?'

Can I answer the question in 3000–4000 words?

You must bear in mind that you need to meet the required word count for your essay. If your question was 'What is your view about the significance of the European Renaissance?', you would require significantly more than 4000 words to answer the question sufficiently. 'What is your view about the importance of Florence in the development of the Renaissance?' would be more manageable.

Settling on the right title

List three possible titles:

1 _____

2 _____

3 _____

For each of the titles that you have written above, you will need to ask yourself some key questions. This will help you decide which title to ultimately go with. Take the first possible title and work your way through the questions. Once you have answered the questions do the same for the other two possible titles:

1 Does it involve assessing a historical concept (e.g. cause, consequence, significance)? Which one?

Title 1: _____

Title 2: _____

Title 3: _____

2 Is there a discussion possible? Explain what it is.

Title 1: _____

Title 2: _____

Title 3: _____

3 Are there different historical views from named historians? How many views are there?

Title 1: _____

Title 2: _____

Title 3: _____

4 Is this a genuine historical topic rather than a topic which involves mainly other disciplines (such as literary criticism)? Explain why.

Title 1: _____

Title 2: _____

Title 3: _____

5 Does it make assumptions (e.g. 'What is your view about why Napoleon was such as bad ruler?') rather than opening up discussion?

Title 1: _____

Title 2: _____

Title 3: _____

6 Are you going to enjoy working with this topic? Explain your reason.

Title 1: _____

Title 2: _____

Title 3: _____

My Progress

Having applied these questions to all of your potential titles you should now have one you feel most confident in pursuing. Write down in the space below the title you want to go ahead with:

My title: _____

Now provide a short explanation about why your chosen title is suitable:

_____

2.3 Compiling resources

Where to start

You have decided on a title and you are now going to begin your research. You will need to find three interpretations and acquire as much contextual knowledge as possible. However interesting your question, if you cannot access this evidence, then you won't be able to meet the requirements of the mark scheme.

Let's say that you have chosen the following question:

> Historians have disagreed about the causes of the Bolshevik seizure of power in Russia in October 1917. What is your view about the causes of the Bolshevik seizure of power in Russia in October 1917?

There is a clear discussion possible here. Initial reading has led you to a series of possible explanations:

- The leadership of Lenin
- The weaknesses of the Provisional Government
- Kerensky's mistakes
- The wider impact of the First World War.

You will be looking for two types of evidence:

1 Interpretations from historians that may form your three chosen works

2 Evidence that could support or contradict the views of different historians.

It might be that within your school or college's history department there are textbooks or academic books and papers about the October Revolution. It might be that the school library contains relevant resources. However, it might be the case that this is a topic that has caught your interest and imagination and does not feature in your school's curriculum.

What to look for when compiling resources

It is important that your chosen works are of article or chapter length, but your supplementary reading can be shorter than this. Popular or TV historians can be used as long as they provide an interpretation that is based on detailed research. One tell-tale sign of quality historical scholarship is the use of references. Does the author reference the work of other historians and research in the course of their work? It is still possible to use a work that does not explicitly use a referencing system but you will need to ensure that the argument is not based solely on personal opinion.

Internet research

Basic research using a search engine will inevitably throw up a mixture of academic and more questionable evidence. This is a good way of ensuring that there is enough material but makes it difficult to assess which works are historically sound. More scholarly search engines such as JSTOR can be frustrating to use as you will inevitably run into paywalls and you may find interfaces that are difficult to navigate, but there are more user-friendly alternatives discussed below and on page 16.

Academic search engines

BASE (Bielefeld Academic Search Engine)
BASE (base-search.net) provides a search engine for academic papers, many of which are open access and free to read.

JURN
JURN (jurn.org) provides a search engine for entirely free and open access academic articles. Its database is updated regularly.

Audiovisual resources

Apple podcasts
Thousands of history podcasts – many of which have been created by recognised academic historians – are available for free on iTunes.

Other podcasts
There are many more podcasts to be found on the internet. Those found on the BBC podcasts website (bbc.co.uk/podcasts), History Extra (historyextra.com) and Historical Association Podcasts (history.org.uk/podcasts) are particularly useful. Remember that any audiovisual materials you use must be produced by recognised historians.

Compiling meaningful resources

Consider the resources (books, websites, magazine articles, etc.) that you have come across so far. Categorise your resources using the table below:

Category	Resources
Resources to help teachers plan lessons rather than serious research	
Resources aimed at Key Stage 3 or lower	
Resources that attempt to break new ground by carrying out innovative research	
Entertainment pieces (e.g. a newspaper article that simply sums up the basics of the topic)	
Books written by recognised historians but intended for the general reader	
Resources that use a lot of references and are clearly aimed at the academic community	
A level textbooks	

Which of these categories would you immediately discount and which are more valuable to the coursework?

_____

_____

_____

What kind of resources would you use first and why?

_____

_____

_____

My Progress

Having completed the activity above, now is your chance to map out your own work on finding resources. If, on reflection, you have found it difficult to locate enough resources for your topic, don't be afraid to change your title if you think another will enable you to find more to work with. As you are still in the early stages of your project it is better to make changes now rather than struggle later on when it might be too late to change. My provisional title:

_____

_____

Are there enough resources accessible for me to continue with this title?

_____

List below the different interpretations on the issue (there should be at least three).

_____

_____

_____

_____

2.4 Starting the research and deciding on your three chosen works

Books

Remember that as well as your three works you are expected to refer to other supplementary reading, so even if you decide a book is not suitable as one of your chosen works, your research will not be wasted. You might be able to find entire books devoted to your topic but your task may be more manageable if you use chapters in books dedicated to wider subject matter. For example, if your question is about different interpretations of the causes of the Spanish Civil War in 1936, a book about Spain in the wider period 1931–1975 will likely contain a chapter about the causes of the war.

Journals and magazines

You can use articles in academic journals, but do bear in mind that these will probably be aimed at the academic community rather than A-level students. *The Historical Journal*, *Journal of British Studies* and *Economic History Review* are some of the many journals that contain peer-reviewed, research-based articles on a wide variety of historical topics.

Articles in magazines more suited to A-level students can be referred to. These include:

- *History Today* – aims to present serious history to a wide audience.
- *History Review* – withdrawn from publication in 2012 but aimed at A-level students. The archive can be found on the *History Today* website.
- *Modern History Review* – managed by a team from the History Department at the University of Warwick, this magazine aims to widen the horizons of A-level students by proving accessible articles by leading scholars.

Google Books and Google Scholar

A good way to start internet research is by using Google Books (books.google.co.uk) and Google Scholar (scholar.google.co.uk). This will provide you with access to previews, **bibliographies** and sometimes entire books, and will give you an idea of the nature of the debate and which leads to follow up.

More precise search terms will give you better results. For example, a search for "interpretations of the Russian Revolution" will produce results like this:

These results may be adequate but will tend to be more generic. A more precise search term, in this case "Weaknesses of the Provisional Government"+"October Revolution" will provide similar results to these:

More precise search terms will provide you with more relevant results and may help you to narrow down your shortlist of chosen works.

Keeping a record of research

When you submit your coursework you will also provide a resource record containing a list of all the research you have done. It is a good idea to begin compiling the resource record early, starting as soon as you do some initial reading around the topic.

My progress

Complete the table below as a record of your initial research.

Date	Author, title and page number	What is the main focus of the work?	What is convincing about the work?	What is less convincing about the work?	Useful as a chosen or supplementary work? Why?

Section 3 Working with interpretations

3.1 What are interpretations?

Much of what we understand about the past is based on our interpretation of it. The photograph below is of the monument at the site of the Battle of Naseby, which took place in Northamptonshire in 1645 during the English Civil War between the Royalist forces of Charles I and the Parliamentarians, led by Thomas Fairfax. Constructed in 1936, the monument bears an inscription that reads, 'from near this site Oliver Cromwell led the Cavalry charge which decided the issue of the battle and ultimately that of the Great Civil War'. In erecting this monument, those involved in its commission and construction made a number of interpretations about the past:

- The sheer fact that a monument was constructed at all demonstrates that a particular interpretation of the past was prevalent at the time. It was felt by those who constructed it that this battle was enough of a turning point to merit a permanent memorial.
- It gives weight to the specific role of Oliver Cromwell rather than other battlefield commanders present on the day.
- It refers to the conflict as the 'Great Civil War'. This suggests that it was of historical and national significance.

Someone else studying the battle may view it very differently.

- If you were an Irish Catholic you might view the monument as a representation of the beginning of Cromwell's rule and the subsequent oppression of Ireland through his military campaigns there.
- If you were involved in archival research for a PhD thesis and found compelling evidence that another battle was in fact the key turning point in the war, you may feel that a monument at the site is unnecessary.
- If you were involved in historical research that focuses on conflicts in the rest of Britain – rather than just in England – in the 1630s and 1640s, you might come to the conclusion that the term 'Great Civil War' is misleading.

From this we can begin to see why different historians form different interpretations of the same events. A particular interpretation of the past may be formed for a number of reasons:

- The focus of a historian's research.
- The questions historians are addressing.
- The chronology historians are studying.
- The kind of evidence the historian is working with.

My Progress

Answer the following questions in order to ascertain why different historians will have contrasting views of your own research question.

1   What is your coursework question?

_____

2   List three possible interpretations of your question.

_____

_____

_____

_____

_____

3   Jot down below the possible reasons why historians have come to these contrasting views. (You can use the bullet points at the bottom of page 18 to help with your thinking.) This may act as the basis for your **criteria** in measuring how strong the **arguments** of each historian are. Some ideas to get you thinking include:

- Historians often spell out their **assumptions**, the questions they are focusing on and the resources they are using in their introduction.
- We can guess the chronological focus from some titles.
- We can guess the emphasis of historians from titles, for example, a book entitled *Why the North won* is likely to focus on the strengths of the North; a book entitled *Why the South lost* is likely to focus on the weaknesses of the South.

_____

_____

_____

_____

_____

_____

_____

_____

_____

_____

_____

_____

_____

_____

3.2 Why do historians come to different conclusions?

Criteria

As we have seen on page 18, historians will place varying emphasis on the importance of an event, individual, place or idea based on criteria that they establish. In the case of the battlefield monument those who constructed it felt that Cromwell was a driving force in instigating change and the battle was of major significance. The criteria they used when deciding if the event was significant includes how important the role of key commanders was and how far it changed the course of the war. It is important to remember that there is no generic set of criteria that should be used when answering all historical questions and it will vary depending on the period, theme, enquiry and evidence being studied.

Establishing criteria: the most important historical site in your home town

In order to begin thinking like a historian it is useful to practise establishing criteria for a specific question. For example, imagine you were answering the question, 'What is the most important historical site in your home town?' A range of possible answers could be put forward to this question.

Resident 1

'I think the **church** is the most important site because as far as I know, it is the oldest building in the town (built in 1450) and therefore it helps us to trace the entire history of the town and the people who have lived in it. It was also where our most famous former resident – an engineer who built bridges all over the country in the nineteenth century – was baptised.'

Resident 2

'I think the **canal** that runs through the town (built in 1830) is the most important site. This is because it was used to transport coal from the nearby colliery in much greater amounts than would have been possible previously. This led to economic prosperity and growth.'

Resident 3

'I think the **railway station** is the most important site because before it was built in 1840, the town was very small and its economy relied almost solely on agriculture. After the station was built, communication improved and new people moved in. It is still important today because commuters rely on it to get to work.'

The three residents have come to different conclusions because they have used different criteria.

- Resident 1 has decided that **age** is an important criterion. The older something is, the more significant it is. They also value **wider impact** outside the town as important, as was the case with the bridge engineer baptised in the church.
- Resident 2 has used **economic impact** and prosperity as their criteria.
- Resident 3 has also used economic impact as a criterion but has decided that they would also take into account how important a site is **today** when deciding its value.

Criteria and coursework

From the exercise above we can see why different people might come to different conclusions when asked the same question. When analysing your chosen works it is important to establish why the three historians have alternate views, and establishing the criteria they have used is a vital place to start. You also need to establish your own criteria when deciding which of the chosen works is most credible.

Establishing criteria

Answer the following questions in order to help you select the criteria you would use when assessing which site in your home town is most important.

1 What is the most important historical site in your home town/village/city?

_____

2 Why is this the most important site?

_____

_____

_____

_____

_____

_____

_____

3 Look at your answer to question 2. What criteria did you use when giving value to your chosen site?

_____

_____

_____

_____

_____

_____

_____

4 Would anyone else you know choose a different site? Why is this? Why might they use different criteria to you?

_____

_____

_____

_____

_____

_____

_____

_____

3.3 How to select and reject interpretations

There would be little value in using an interpretation in your coursework if it did not clearly present a view that can be **corroborated** and challenged. If it simply states facts it would not be very useful to use as an interpretation.

Look at Extract 1 below, taken from an A level textbook. This extract and the one on page 23 could be used in the coursework enquiry **'What is your view about whether Italy was a great power under Mussolini in the years 1935–43?'**

Extract 1: A. Mitchell and G. Stewart, *The Collapse of the Liberal State and the Triumph of Fascism in Italy, 1896–1943* (2011)

Mussolini carried out a state visit to Germany in September 1937 and was impressed by increasing German might. In November, he joined the Anti-Comintern Pact, linking Italy, Germany and Japan in a grouping aimed on the surface at the Soviet Union but, in many ways, at British interests too. In March 1938, Hitler invaded and annexed Austria, bringing the Third Reich to the Italian border. Hitler claimed that he would never forget Mussolini's acceptance of this. In reality, however, Mussolini was now tied to Germany as the junior partner. At the Munich Conference in September, Mussolini promoted peace because Italy was not ready for war, but in every way he championed Germany's interests.

This extract certainly provides us with useful information for the enquiry. It tells us that Mussolini attempted to bring Italy into a closer alliance with Hitler's Germany and in the process became the inferior nation. There is nothing wrong with the extract. It is accurate and certainly useful for a student preparing for an exam on Mussolini's Italy or indeed looking for contextual information for this coursework enquiry. What the extract does not do is form its own detailed interpretation of the evidence put forward, which we would not expect from an A level text. For this reason it would not be sensible to use this as one of your chosen works.

Suitable extracts

Why do you think this extract is not suitable to use as a chosen work? What would you expect from more suitable works?

_____

_____

_____

_____

Selecting interpretations

Read Extract 2 and identify the interpretation being put forward, together with the criteria the author has used in order to form their view.

Extract 2: J. Whittam, *Fascist Italy* (1995)

When the Duce [Mussolini] visited Germany in September 1937 he found Nazi power a much more compelling argument; in November he joined the Anti-Comintern Pact and in December he withdrew from the League of Nations. Diplomatically and ideologically, the Duce appeared to have made his choice. He had turned his back on the democracies and opted for the Axis.

The intervention in Spain [on Franco's side in the Civil War] had never been popular with the Italian people, especially as it seemed to lead to closer collaboration with Germany. The racial laws [similar to those found in Nazi Germany] ... indicated subservience. Asserting Italy's great power status by humiliating the British and French was, ironically, converting her into the satellite of Nazi Germany. The Czech Crisis [when a European war was narrowly avoided after the British agreed to Germany annexing part of Czechoslovakia] of the summer and autumn of 1938 at least offered Mussolini the appearance of being independent. With Europe on the brink of war after Chamberlain's failure to reach an agreement ... the Duce welcomed the chance to emerge as a mediator. To the outside world it was Mussolini who had persuaded Hitler to meet with Chamberlain ... He was in fact merely aiding and abetting the Nazi leader. It was, however, 'peace in our time' and the Duce had played his part, even if the script had been written in German.

1   What is the overarching argument of the extract? Summarise this in one sentence.

_____

_____

_____

2   What evidence has the author put forward in coming to this view?

_____

_____

_____

_____

3   What criteria has the author used when making their judgement about how far Italy was a great power?

_____

_____

_____

_____

3.4 Identifying the aim of an author

One reason why historians come to different conclusions is because they may have conflicting aims when carrying out their research. Imagine, for example, two historians have researched the causes of the First World War.

- One historian might start with the aim of finding out what role German imperial ambitions had in causing the war. This would lead them to seek out sources related to this, perhaps in German archives and perhaps never published before, which might support the argument that German imperial ambition was the most important cause.
- If a historian embarked on research with the aim of finding out more about advances in military technology in the early twentieth century, they might conclude that the war started because of increased investment and militarism from the great powers.

Therefore, in order to help you understand why the authors of your chosen works have formed contrasting views, it is useful to begin by determining what their aim was in carrying out their research.

Read the extract below and the commentary.

Extract 1: E. P. Thompson, *The Making of the English Working Class* (1968)

The question, of course, is how the individual got to be in this 'social role', and how the particular social organization (with its property-rights and structure of authority) got to be there. And these are historical questions. If we stop history at a given point, then there are no classes but simply a multitude of individuals with a multitude of experiences. But if we watch these men over an adequate period of social change, we observe patterns in their relationships, their ideas, and their institutions. Class is defined by men as they live their own history, and, in the end, this is its only definition.

The ultimate aim of this work is to establish how the class system was formed.

The author aims to track development over an extended period of time.

I am convinced that we cannot understand class unless we see it as a social and cultural formation, arising from processes which can only be studied as they work themselves out over a considerable historical period. In the years between 1780 and 1832 most English working people came to feel an identity of interests as between themselves and as against their rulers and employers.

The author aims to track this process from 1780 to 1832 and relate it to the issue of class.

The aims of an author

How does knowing the aim of an author help us understand their interpretation?

_____

_____

_____

_____

_____

_____

_____

_____

Read the extract below. What is the aim of the book? Provide as much detail as possible.

Extract 2: Joanna Arman, *The Warrior Queen: The Life and Legend of Aethelflaed, Daughter of Alfred the Great* (2017)

In literature and fiction, Æthelflæd is often cast as the archetypal warrior queen, but also as a frustrated wife trapped in a loveless arranged marriage who seeks romantic fulfilment elsewhere … Leaving aside the tropes of romantic fiction, and the mythologising of past ages, is it possible to learn something of the real Æthelflæd? We do not have a full-length biography of her like the *Life of Alfred*, which was written for her father by the Welsh monk Asser. As a consequence, the contemporary sources have little to say about her childhood and early life. When she enters the historical record in the *Anglo-Saxon Chronicle*, it is as an adult in her forties, and she is dead within a few years. Such is the nature of this source, with its terse narrative style, reporting major events with only brief entries. It is little wonder that 'other contemporary sources' are included with the best-known modern edition of Asser's *Life of Alfred* – to truly get to know him, and learn about his life and career, it is sometimes necessary to read between the lines and consult other available sources, such as charters, legal codes and writings from neighbouring kingdoms. Thus, to see the bigger picture of Alfred's life it is necessary to look at the wider context of his times, and his relations with his family and contemporaries. It is only sensible to assume that the same applies to his daughter.

She too was a product of her times. Her life was dominated by the conflict with the Danish and Norwegian Vikings. Her father's kingdom was the last to stand alone against their onslaught, and it is possible that her uncle, King Æthelred, died as a result of a military engagement against them. In this sense, it was the war with the Danes that made Alfred king and placed his family on the political and military stage. Æthelflæd was probably born only a year or so before her father succeeded the throne of Wessex, and she would have been raised at his court. For this reason, it is possible to discover something about how she spent the first sixteen or so years of her life from examining the actions and movements of her family, who must have shared many experiences with their patriarch. For instance, Alfred's wife and children almost certainly accompanied him into his famous exile in the Somerset marshes. At the time Æthelflæd would have been around seven or eight years old – old enough to remember that desperate time when all seemed lost, and to remember her father's legendary victory at Edington, when his great enemy Guthrum was defeated and he won back his kingdom. She would not, of course, have fought in the battle, but she would certainly have known about it, and it had a very real impact on her family. In the years following the battle she would have been educated alongside her older siblings, and it is hard to believe that a young girl of keen intelligence and ability (these features would be displayed later in her life) would not have observed her father, and learned from him the rudiments of rule and statecraft.

_____

_____

_____

_____

_____

_____

_____

_____

_____

_____

_____

_____

3.5 Identifying arguments in interpretations

Identifying arguments in interpretations and distinguishing these from factual evidence is vital. It is also useful to establish whether sufficient and accurate evidence has been presented to support any arguments. If an interpretation makes assertions without backing these up with evidence the author would not be practising good history.

Look at the example below that distinguishes between interpretation and evidence in two extracts. The examples come from interpretations that could be used in the coursework enquiry '**What is your view about how successful Margaret Thatcher's government was in the years 1979–90?**'

Interpretation

Evidence

Extract 1: Selina Todd, *The People: The Rise and Fall of the Working Class* (2014)

In 1984 the Government's determination to destroy the labour movement was made starkly clear. In February Ian MacGregor, head of the National Coal Board (NCB) announced plans to close twenty pits with the loss of 20,000 jobs – often in areas that offered little alternative employment. On 12 March 1984, Arthur Scargill, president of the national Union of Mineworkers (NUM) called a national strike against the closures.

When explaining her reforms, Margaret Thatcher was fond of invoking the so-called 'TINA' phrase: 'There is no alternative'. But in the case of the miners, there was an alternative. It did not make economic sense to close the mines. The Oxford economist Andrew Glyn convincingly argued that even if the pits were as uneconomic (and in fact many still had sufficient resources to merit mining for decades to come) the resulting unemployment would oblige the NCB and the taxpayer funding larger retirement pensions, thousands of redundancy payments and millions of pounds in unemployment benefit. It was cheaper to keep the miners in work.

The decision to close the mines was politically motivated and had a long history.

Extract 2: Terrence Casey (ed), *The Social Context of Economic Change in Britain* (2012)

On numerous measures Britain's relative performance since 1979 has been on a par with – and in some respects even superior to – that of other G7* economies. Improved relative performance has not been sufficient, however, to close the absolute gaps in income and productivity arising from decades of decline. The long-term trend of economic decline bottomed out under Conservative economic stewardship, but the Tories were unable to reverse the process. Even if the Conservatives did not meet their stated goals, halting the process of decline was a major feat. The period of Conservative rule thus represents a positive improvement in the trajectory of the British economy.

Indeed, the Conservatives' economic legacy would probably be more widely praised had it not been for the 1990–92 recession, which seriously marred an otherwise favourable record. Hard won economic gains, particularly on inflation and employment, evaporated – which critics took to indicate the shallowness of the economic improvements. In reality the economy was allowed to overheat in the 1980s, but the supply side improvements were real.

*Group of the world's seven most industrialised economies (Canada, France, Germany, Italy, Japan, UK, USA)

As you can see, both extracts form interpretations and use evidence in order to back these up.

- The interpretation given in Extract 1 is that the government was wrong to close down the mines and is generally negative about Thatcher.
- The interpretation given in Extract 2 is that the economy improved and is generally positive about Thatcher.

As with any historian aiming to present an argument, they both use evidence that assists the case they are presenting. The kind of evidence used by a historian is something to look out for when analysing your chosen works.

Read the following extracts. Use two different colours to highlight a) the argument or interpretation and b) the evidence used.

Extract 3: Ellis Wasson, *A History of Modern Britain* (2009)

For some, Thatcher was a figure of Churchillian stature, a savior who altered the course of Britain. She took command of a derelict wreck, ready to sink, and guided it not just to safe harbor but to repair, relaunching, and a new beginning. Her accomplishments were prodigious, and she led her party to three electoral victories. Her privatization policies took a dramatic turn, the sale of state assets tripled the number of owners of stock between 1979 and 1989. This strategy and war with the unions decisively reshaped the class structure of Britain. 'Thatcherism' split the working class into winners and losers.

However, Thatcher was actually more cautious than she sometimes seemed and less effective in putting many of her ideas into practice than one might expect. She abandoned her initial economic program in 1981 when it clearly was not working. The frontiers of the state, outside the sale of assets, were not rolled back. Welfare and expenditure on healthcare expanded during her tenure.

Extract 4: Earl A. Reitan, *The Thatcher Revolution: Margaret Thatcher, John Major, Tony Blair, and the Transformation of Modern Britain* (2002)

The GLC (Greater London Council), led by 'Red Ken' Livingstone, was Thatcher's thorn in the flesh. From 1981 to 1986 Livingstone increased GLC expenditures by 170 percent. He greatly expanded the number of employees and other dependents and made generous grants to activist groups. He claimed to be creating 'urban socialism' as the people's alternative to Thatcherism. He hung red flags on the GLC building across the Thames from the houses of Parliament, invited foreign revolutionaries to the council chambers, and posted a banner listing the figures for unemployment. In 1981, the GLC cut fares on the London Underground by 32 percent, a popular step, and raised the rates to make up the difference. The government intervened and London Transport was nationalized.

Thatcher's answer to urban noncompliance was a demonstration of raw power, fuelled not a little by anger. In 1985, the Thatcher ministry proposed abolition of eighteen urban councils whose fiscal management was regarded as irresponsible. Labour controlled all but two. The list included the six metropolitan counties established by the Heath government plus the GLC.

Which argument is more convincing? Explain your answer.

_____

_____

_____

_____

_____

_____

_____

_____

_____

_____

_____

_____

_____

_____

3.6 Turning arguments into questions

In order to establish what a historian is attempting to achieve in their work, we have already seen that establishing their aim early on is a good idea. It is also helpful to turn their arguments into a series of questions. This can help when you come to explain the differences between your chosen works. See the example below, which could be used in the coursework enquiry '**What is your view about the reasons for the fall of the USSR?**'

Extract 1: Richard Sakwa, *Soviet Politics in Perspective* (1998)

In its final years the Soviet economy faced significant problems, including systemic difficulties arising from problems internal to the socialist economy, and which could be remedied by actions taken by the leadership itself. Most of the latter arose from the pattern of Stalinist super-industrialisation which created a vast top-heavy bureaucracy managing the country's economic life. At a certain stage the enormous costs and wastage involved in maintaining the managing mechanism, the heart of the command economy, condemned Soviet-type economies to relative stagnation. In the absence of the invisible hand of capitalist market forces, and the increasingly palsied condition of the visible hand of command planning, such economies had no self-sustaining mechanism to imbue them with dynamism. These problems were not new, and the issue of economic reform had been at or near the top of the agenda at least since the death of Stalin.

In Extract 1, the author could be seen to be posing the following questions:

1. What problems did the Soviet economy face in its final years?

2. What was the impact of Stalinist super-industrialisation?

3. How did the Soviet economy cope without capitalism?

Extract 2: Paul R. Gregory, *The Political Economy of Stalinism* (2004)

The Soviet administrative-command economy continued to have positive economic growth until 1989. The negative growth thereafter is indicative of an economic system in collapse. Although the USSR began the postwar era with high rates of growth (which were matched by much of Europe and exceeded by the economic miracles in Germany and Japan), its growth declined steadily after 1970. Whereas growth in Western industrialized economies turned down in response to energy crises in the mid-1970s and early 1980s, they bounced back so that no long-term declining trend was evident.

The fateful decision in favour of radical economic reform was not forced by outright collapse. The party elite were reasonably satisfied, and the Soviet population was not in open opposition. The administrative command system, on the eve of its radical change, was inefficient but stable. Gosplan's projections called for an annual growth rate of some 3 percent through the year 2000. Declining Soviet growth rate, coupled with the acceleration of growth in China, Southeast Asia, and the marked recovery of the U.S. economy, were troubling but do not fully explain the fateful steps that eventually spelled the demise of the system.

In Extract 2, the author could be seen to be posing the following questions:

1. How did the Soviet economy perform in comparison to major Western nations?

2. How successful was the Soviet administrative command system in the late 1980s?

3. Why did the system collapse?

If a historian's argument is turned into the questions they seem to be asking, it can be much easier to distinguish between arguments and see clearly what the aim of their research is.

Read the extracts below and repeat the activity on page 28, identifying the questions that the authors seem to be asking. The extracts could be used in the coursework enquiry '**What is your view about whether there was a crisis in late Elizabethan government (1589–1603)?**'

Extract 3: Ian W. Archer, *The Pursuit of Stability: Social Relations in Elizabethan London* (2003)

People's fears in later Elizabethan England did have some grounding in reality, and the evidence that crime was committed by organised gangs was growing in the later 1580s and 1590s, because of the problem of disbanded soldiers. Their identification with crime was a commonplace well before the continuous war of the closing years of the century. The habits of violence soldiers had acquired in the wars were compounded by the difficulties of reintegrating with civilian society, particularly in circumstances of rising unemployment and dearth. It was therefore often only by crime that the discharged soldier was able to support himself, and the protests of the privy council against the gangs of highway robbers and burglars terrorising the city and its environs become a depressing theme of its correspondence in the 1590s, as waves of discharged soldiers repeatedly hit the south coast ports and headed for London.

What kinds of questions does the author of Extract 3 seem to be asking?

_____

_____

_____

_____

_____

Extract 4: B. Kane and V. McGowan-Doyle, *Elizabeth I and Ireland* (2014), Cambridge University Press

Unlike some of her subjects, Elizabeth had a fairly well-developed ability to interpret Ireland from a culturally relativist point of view. At a time when official policy was to confine the Irish churches to using either English or Latin, Elizabeth showed an interest in Gaelic … Elizabeth had some grasp of Irish culture, or at least of the fact that the Irish possessed a distinct culture as opposed to an absence of culture. She was frequently inclined to pardon Irish rebels so long as she was not 'touched in her honour' and so long as her clemency was not mistaken for weakness … Elizabeth described herself as married to her realm, but in Ireland she was a distant figure, and her authority even over her own deputies, let alone her Old English or Gaelic subjects, was arguably more tenuous because of her gender.

What kinds of questions does the author of Extract 4 seem to be asking?

_____

_____

_____

_____

_____

_____

_____

_____

3.7 Identifying and explaining differences between works

In order to satisfy bullet point 3 of the mark scheme (see pages 7–9) you are required to show an understanding of the reasons for the contrasting views found in your chosen works. Through this you are expected to show an understanding of the basis of the arguments of the authors. Sections 3.8 and 3.9 on evaluation and selection of criteria will help you to do this but one important reason why historians form different arguments is their use of source material.

It is important to note that different works may not be diametrically opposed (at completely opposite extremes), and it is not unusual to find common ground between them. Therefore, it is worth considering similarities and differences in interpretation, as well as discovering ways in which works may be different but compatible.

The following extracts could be used in the coursework enquiry '**What is your view about how far religious differences were responsible for the outbreak of the English Civil War?**'

Extract 1: B.G. Blackwood, 'Parties and Issues in the Civil War in Lancashire' in *Transactions of the Historic Society of Lancashire and Cheshire* (1982)

A superficial reading of the source material might lead us to suppose that the Lancashire farmers had strong Royalist leanings during the Civil War. In the Royalist Composition papers eighty-nine yeomen and seventy husbandmen are named as having supported the King. In a list of just over 1,000 suspected Lancashire Royalists drawn up by Major-General Charles Worsley in 1655 208 yeomen and 343 husbandmen are recorded. Even allowing for underestimates, these figures of peasant support for Royalism are not impressive, especially as there must have been, at the very least, 8,000 peasant families in Lancashire in 1642 … The surviving Protestation returns also suggest that the peasantry were less politically and, more arguably, less religiously conservative than the gentry.

Extract 2: Christopher Hibbert, *Cavaliers and Roundheads: The English Civil War 1642–1649* (1993)

The Cornish squire Sir Bevil Grenville, grandson of Queen Elizabeth's admiral, 'a lover of learning and a genial host', who had many friends amongst the Parliamentarians and was to die fighting bravely against them, said … 'I cannot contain myself within my doors when the King of England's standard waves in the field, the cause being such as to make all that die in it little inferior to martyrs' … For men like Bevil Grenville it was not only that the King's majesty was sacrosanct, there was also the belief that the King was the defender of the true Church.

It is clear from these extracts that the authors have used quite different source material and as a result have made contrasting judgements about the circumstances that started the Civil War.

- Blackwood has used the Royalist Composition Papers and a list of suspected Lancashire Royalists drawn up after the war. Through this he has attempted to identify the role of peasants in the outbreak of war.
- Hibbert has clearly used narrative sources, such as letters and diaries. His focus is on the role of the gentry and upper classes, so it is no surprise that he has come to a different conclusion to Blackwood.

Of course, there are a number of other possible reasons why your chosen works might contain different views. These include:

- The questions the historians are asking of the material might be different.
- Their own research focus may be different (they might have contrasting aims).
- They might be studying different chronologies or time periods.
- They might have used different criteria when assessing the importance of an event or individual.
- They might be writing under different intellectual frameworks; the time they were writing in and the sources available to them at the time might influence their interpretation.

My progress

Using two extracts that you have found for your coursework enquiry, complete the grid below.

Key similarities between chosen works	Why are there similarities?

Key differences between your chosen works	Why do they have different views?

3.8 Applying knowledge to interpretations

A key determining factor in achieving higher marks in your coursework is how successfully you integrate a sound knowledge of the **debate** into your argument. A good way to do this is to integrate knowledge into your discussion of interpretations throughout your essay. It is likely that you already have experience in this skill from your Paper 1 Section C interpretations topic. In general, you need to remember the following when applying knowledge to your interpretations:

- The knowledge that you apply to the interpretations must be accurate and relevant to the issue.
- It must be linked to the interpretation to show it supports or challenges the view in the interpretation.
- Large amounts of knowledge should not simply follow after an interpretation with no comment suggesting whether that knowledge makes the view of the interpretation more or less valid.
- The link between the interpretation and the own knowledge should come through evaluative words or phrases (see box below).

As this is not an examined unit and you will have all resources available to you during the write-up process, it might be expected that the quality of your own knowledge and evaluation is better than that used in your examination topics when you do not have your books to hand.

Although it might appear rather mechanical it would be greatly useful to build up a working list of evaluative words and phrases that you can call upon when writing your essay.

Evaluative words and phrases

Words

However

Conversely

Although

Opposes

Illustrates

Confirms

Endorses

Refutes

Phrases

This is supported by …

This is challenged by …

The view is valid because …

The view is questionable because …

The interpretation can be criticised …

The view can be exemplified with the example of …

On the other hand …

His argument rests on the premise that … however …

Too much significance is given to … whereas …

The historian makes a generalisation that excludes …

There is sometimes no evidence to support a claim, such as …

Consider the following question and the interpretation that a model student has found:

What is your view about how much support there was for the English Church on the eve of the Reformation?

Extract 1: A.G. Dickens, *The English Reformation* (1964)

Anti-clericalism had reached a new intensity by the early years of the sixteenth century, attitudes towards monasticism were muted and support for monasteries commanded little support outside the cloister. Clerical power and influence in society was more apparent than was the case in practice. The clergy were beginning to lose their intellectual and educational dominance. They might stand in a favourable position to wage any conflict against the growing threat of the laity and of the State, but their leaders lacked inspiration, unity and loyalty to the supranational [across international borders] concept of Christendom. The English Church remained too full of conflicting self-interest to bring about its own reform.

Having worked out what the view of the interpretation is about the issue in the question, consider the two following attempts to evaluate the view Dickens offers.

Response A

Dickens argues that the English Church on the eve of the Reformation was in a weak position. He puts forward the view that there was little support for monasticism, while clerical influence was also on the decline. He explains this decline as being due to the loss of the educational and intellectual dominance of the clergy. He suggests that the leaders of the clergy were not inspirational and were divided, suggesting that they would be unable to defend the Church should it come under attack. Dickens firmly believes that the Church lacked popular support.

Response B

Although Dickens has argued that the Church lacked popular support, with both monasticism and clerical influence in decline, his view is not entirely accurate. While he is correct to note the numbers entering the monasteries dropping as the monastic ideal lost its appeal, he is far from correct to argue that there was a decline in clerical influence or appeal. Dickens' view ignores the 1520s when laymen entered the priesthood in numbers only ever exceeded in the previous decade and there was little evidence of clashes between priests and laity. It is very unlikely that large numbers of men would join an institution that was in decline and under serious attack from the laity.

What is the difference between the two responses?

_____

Which of these responses simply describes Dickens' view?

_____

Which one of these responses evaluates Dickens' view?

_____

Which evaluative words are used?

_____

Identify and highlight where the own knowledge is directly linked to the interpretation.

_____

My progress

Fill in the tables on the next two pages for each of your chosen works in order to ascertain which knowledge can be used to support and challenge the views in your chosen works.

Chosen work 1

	Key arguments	Knowledge that supports this argument	Knowledge that challenges this argument
Key argument 1			
Key argument 2			
Key argument 3			

My progress continued

Chosen work 2

	Key arguments	Knowledge that supports this argument	Knowledge that challenges this argument
Key argument 1			
Key argument 2			
Key argument 3			

Chosen work 3

	Key arguments	Knowledge that supports this argument	Knowledge that challenges this argument
Key argument 1			
Key argument 2			
Key argument 3			

3.9 Applying criteria to interpretations

The fourth bullet point in the mark scheme refers to how successfully you have established criteria by which your interpretations can be judged and how effectively these criteria have been applied (see pages 7–9). It is important that your work fulfils all aspects of the mark scheme in order to achieve your optimum grade and this is one that should not be overlooked. It is important to note that establishing these criteria is not something that can be taught in the traditional sense and it will vary depending on the topic you have chosen and the interpretations you have used. Read the example below and complete the 'My progress' task on pages 38–39 in order to begin establishing your own criteria.

Example

A student has chosen the question '**What is your view about how far ordinary Germans supported the Holocaust?**'

Sensible criteria for a question such as this might include:

1   Whether the historian has researched a broad cross-section of German society rather than a few individuals.

2   Whether the historian has used statistical evidence to back up their findings (for example, figures of how many Germans volunteered to join the SS versus those who were conscripted), and how reliable these statistics are.

3   Whether the historian has used accounts from ordinary Germans.

4   Whether other available evidence supports or contradicts the findings of the historian.

Below is an extract from one of the chosen works.

Extract 1: Christopher Browning, *Ordinary Men: Reserve Police Battalion 101 and the Final Solution in Poland* (1992)

In the very early hours of July 13, 1942, the men of Reserve Police Battalion 101 were roused from their bunks in the large brick school building that served as their barracks in the Polish town of Bilgoraj. They were middle-aged family men of working- and lower-middle-class background from the city of Hamburg. Considered too old to be of use to the German army, they had been drafted instead into the Order Police. Most were raw recruits with no previous experience in German occupied territory. They had arrived in Poland less than three weeks earlier.

Pale and nervous, with choking voice and tears in his eyes, [Commander of the Battalion] Trapp visibly fought to control himself as he spoke. The battalion, he said, plaintively, had to perform a frightfully unpleasant task. This assignment was not to his liking, indeed it was highly regrettable, but the orders came from the highest authorities … The Jews had instigated the American Boycott that had damaged Germany, one policeman remembered Trapp saying. There were Jews in the village who were involved with the partisans, he explained according to two others. The battalion had now been ordered to round up these Jews.

When the men of First Company were summoned to the marketplace, instructed in giving a 'neck shot', and sent to the woods to kill Jews, some of them tried to make up for the opportunity they had missed earlier [to ask to be excused]. One policeman approached First Sergeant Kammer, whom he knew well. He confessed that the task was 'repugnant' to him and asked for a different assignment. Kammer obliged, assigning him to guard duty on the edge of the forest.

This is only a short extract from a much more substantial work, but already we can see how the criteria established above can be applied in order to make a judgement.

The following conclusions can be made when this work is assessed in relation to the criteria established above:

1 The focus of this research is only on one Battalion, so according to the first criterion the usefulness of this work may be brought into question.

2 Browning does use some statistics elsewhere in the book, such as the fact that only 12 of the 500 men in the Battalion refused to fight.

3 The work is based on the accounts of the ordinary Germans in the Battalion, which may satisfy the third criterion somewhat.

4 You may find that research done by other historians backs up Browning's argument that ordinary Germans were essentially following orders and were not particularly passionate about their task.

What is vital to remember is that the criteria used will not be the same for every question or even for two students answering the same question. What is crucial is that you are consistent in your application of criteria and that all three chosen works are given equal treatment and evaluation.

My progress

Write in the space below a list of criteria that could be applied to your chosen works in order to make judgements about their arguments.

_____

_____

_____

_____

_____

_____

_____

_____

_____

_____

_____

_____

_____

_____

_____

_____

_____

_____

_____

➜

My progress continued

For each of your chosen works, write down how well they meet these criteria.

Chosen work 1

→

My progress continued

Chosen work 2

Chosen work 3

Section 4 Writing the essay

4.1 Introduction to writing up

The need to maintain focus

As you have already seen from the other sections of this book, you are not required to learn any new skills but are instead developing those that you already have. As your coursework essay can be much longer than an exam answer, you will also have the opportunity to consider the different ways in which the past has been explained and interpreted.

Historians think that some issues are more important than others in explaining an event and you will need to weigh up, or evaluate, those different interpretations. From your reading, you will have looked at the interpretations of your three chosen works, and you will have thought about the evidence that there is to support or challenge each one. You will have had plenty of time to think about the issues and to find ample relevant and detailed knowledge. No single book will provide you with a ready-made answer: there is no short cut to this, but if you have carried out sufficient research you will be in a position to begin writing up a strong piece of work.

You will need to make sure that you have a thorough understanding of the arguments in your chosen works and evidence to support all sides of the debate in question. As you are doing this, you should keep thinking about the key issues relevant to the question. If you do this you should have a strong line of argument when you write your plan. This should also ensure that you write relevant material for your coursework assignment. You must make sure that everything you write is about the specific controversy in your question and not just about the wider topic.

In general, you need to remember the following throughout the writing-up process:

- You will need to ensure that there are no parts of the answer where you lose focus on the actual question.
- You will need to check that there are no parts where there is just description.
- You need to ensure that you have considered evidence that supports and challenges the different views in your chosen works.
- All of your arguments will need to be backed up by details and accurate knowledge and your conclusion should follow logically from what you have said in the main body of your answer.

When you are ready to begin writing up you will need to have the following available:

- All your reading
- Detailed notes
- Your three chosen works read, analysed, highlighted, etc.
- A range of supplementary reading.

My progress

Complete the planning checklist below. In the 'answer' column, elaborate on your responses.

Question	Answer
Do you have three chosen works selected?	My three chosen works: 1 2 3
Do they provide three contrasting views?	A summary of the contrasting views:
Do you have a range of supplementary reading?	A summary of the supplementary reading acquired:
Do you have detailed notes on the arguments presented in the chosen works?	Key lines of argument in the three chosen works:
Have you established the similarities as well as differences between your chosen works?	A summary of the similarities: A summary of the differences:
Have you established criteria by which your chosen works can be judged?	A summary of my criteria:
Have you established the basis of the historians' arguments?	Basis of arguments:

4.2 Creating a simple essay plan

How will you bring all this together? The best way to do it is to ensure that you have a clear plan. As a starting point it might be helpful to construct a spider diagram that outlines the issues you are going to cover and the key arguments in the chosen works as this will give you the chance to check that you have considered all the issues you need and that they are all relevant to your question.

Let us assume that you have chosen to answer the question:

'What is your view on the reasons why the USA was unable to win the Vietnam War?'

Your spider diagram would provide you with a list of arguments, from your three chosen works, that explain why the USA was unable to win the war, not just a list of events. However, it should also show any links between interpretations and chosen works and it would be helpful, in light of your research, to show the relative importance or weigh up the interpretations so that you have actually assessed the reasons and not simply produced a list. The result might look something like the one below.

You could then indicate beside each view how convincing you found it and why. Ultimately you need to decide which interpretation you found most convincing.

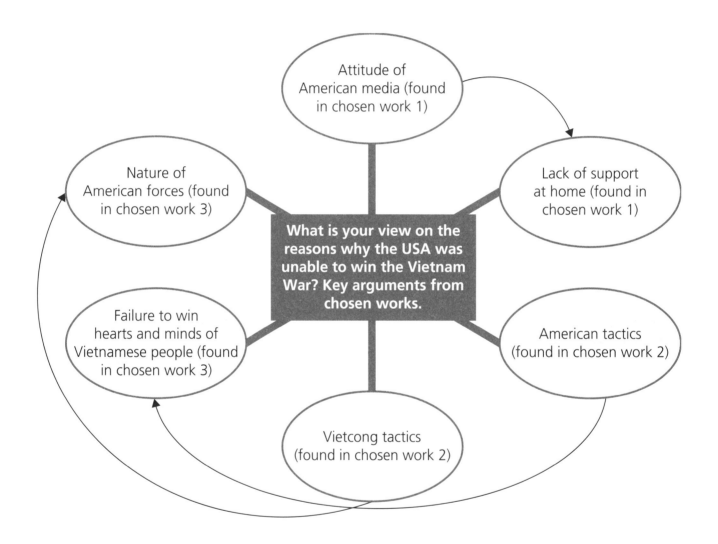

Spider diagram

Construct a spider diagram for your own title showing the issues you are going to consider.

- What are the main interpretations raised by the chosen works?
- What links are there between interpretations?
- How important is each of the issues in answering the question? Put a number by each factor and explain their importance.
- Which is the strongest argument and which is the strongest counter-argument?

4.3 Developing a detailed plan

Providing full coverage of all the issues

The spider diagram that you have created on page 43 will provide you with a basic plan and ensure that you have covered all the issues that are important in answering your question. This section will look at developing the outline into a full plan and checking that you have all the information and materials you will need to be able to start to write it up.

The first stage is to ensure that you have considered all the implications of your question:

- Underline or highlight the key words and phrases in your title, perhaps with the command words in one colour and the key words or phrases in another. This will help you to maintain focus.

On page 43 you identified the issues that you intend to cover in your answer, but now you need:

- an outline of the interpretations you will cover
- evidence to support and challenge each interpretation.

Deciding on a structure

You need to integrate information from the chosen works and other factual knowledge into your argument. Your plan should identify which approach to this you are going to take. You have a number of options:

- You could write an essay of continuous prose, without subheadings. You need to ensure you are able to explain, analyse and compare the chosen works while integrating your own knowledge into your argument. You could write the essay issue-by-issue or work-by-work.
- You could write an initial section discussing the key issues and debates, followed by an assessment of your three chosen works. You could use subheadings to divide up your sections.
- You could simply write under subheadings for your three chosen works.
- You might find it useful to write down in the margin on this page which structure you want to use and why.

No structure is superior to any other, and it is important to remember that what you need to provide is an organised, evaluative answer that fulfils the requirements of the mark scheme.

You need to reach a **judgement** on the controversy and ultimately decide which of the chosen works provides the most persuasive interpretation.

You might find it easier to plan your answer by using a chart with a series of columns like the one on page 45.

My progress

Create a chart like the one below. You can complete it on this page or reproduce it on a large sheet of paper.

Issue (Associated chosen work)	Evidence for	Evidence against	Link to other interpretations	How convincing and why
Chosen work 1				
Chosen work 2				
Chosen work 3				
Conclusion:				

4.4 Writing the introduction – what not to do

It is better not to think in terms of an 'introduction' but rather a key opening paragraph that will set out clearly the issues and help the reader to understand your thinking and also help you to develop your arguments purposefully.

Let's take the following question on the French Revolution as an example:

> What is your view on the extent to which Napoleon undermined the gains of the French Revolution?

Napoleon did undermine the gains of the French Revolution, and there is a debate among historians about how far this is true. Sutherland and D.G. Wright agree that Napoleon undermined the gains, while Steven Englund defends Napoleon against his critics. The arguments of those who see Napoleon undermining the Revolution are more convincing. Napoleon's new government proved similar to that of the monarchy of the ancient regime. He restored privilege in respect to wealth, land and law, which undermined the work of the National Assembly. Censorship and repression undermined freedom of expression. Napoleon's Civil Code undermined his call for individual liberty. He restored the powerful position of the Church as his main outlet for spreading the influence of his own power and he destroyed universal male suffrage. His contempt for the constitutions makes Sutherland's view convincing.

There is nothing wrong in stating a view and here it is quite clear what the answer is going to be. However, there are a number of problems with this introduction.

- The terms of reference are not set out. For instance, what were the gains of the Revolution?
- What are the criteria for judgement?
- The title has been chosen because there is an opportunity to explore the debate, but the introduction does not really explain the nature of the debate, so an opportunity is lost.
- Overall, the introduction should present the 'big ideas' that are going to be discussed and give an initial judgement.

On the plus side, this introduction contains a number of positive characteristics.

- The different interpretations in the chosen works are briefly set out, although not in great detail.
- A good understanding is shown of some of the context to the question, although this is brief.
- It does make a judgement about which chosen works are more and less convincing.

Effective introductions

Now that we have considered some key ingredients of a good introduction, look at the sample introduction below and decide whether it is effective or not and why.

What is your view on the extent to which the Spanish Armada was the biggest challenge to the rule of Elizabeth I?

In 1588 Philip II launched a formidable Armada against England and this was the biggest external challenge the Queen had faced. Elizabeth had tried to maintain good relations with Spain and had played on the common fears of France and commercial ties. However, relations had become bad because of English raids on Spanish colonies and then English support for Dutch Rebels. The invasion might have had serious consequences if it had been successful so its defeat was very important for Elizabeth and though Spain tried again none of the invasion attempts were successful, a factor given significant weight in Mattingly's work. There were other key elements in Elizabeth's reign like the Settlement of the Church, which Hutchinson claims to be more important, and this essay will compare them with the Armada to decide whether they or the events of 1588 were the defining moment of the reign.

1   Are the key issues or wording of the question explained?

_____

_____

_____

2   Is there any indication of why there might be different interpretations about the Armada's importance?

_____

_____

_____

3   Are criteria for judgement explored?

_____

_____

_____

4   What do you think the writer's own view is?

_____

_____

_____

4.5 Writing the introduction – what to do

Let's have a look at another sample introduction, this time on the following question:

> What is your view on the extent to which Marshall Aid was merely a policy of American self-interest?

The US presented Marshall Aid as a policy aimed to help the recovery of Europe. However, it has been claimed by Jeremy Isaacs that there were ulterior motives and that self-interest rather than a disinterested concern for Europe was the key to the policy. This self-interest has been seen as creating new European trade links to benefit the US economy, as Kennedy-Pipe has made clear, the USA were primarily concerned with the 'search for new markets'.

However, the Soviet view was that this was dollar diplomacy merely intended to increase US influence in Europe. S.J. Ball sees Marshall more intent to block off 'the Soviet Union's expansion' while Jeremy Isaacs casts doubt on the idealism of Marshall Aid by pointing out that much of the aid in practice went straight back to the USA. It is useful when measuring these interpretations to assess how far the Americans benefited, both economically and politically. It could be said that the US was concerned with global politics and the need to restrict the spread of Communism, but was also keen to show that traditional ethical concerns were at the heart of US policy.

In this introduction, the key ideas are presented more clearly – the notion of self-interest is set against strategic and economic interests, and the views of the chosen works are neatly summarised. There is a hint at an overall judgement at the end, that self-interest and humanitarian concerns were not necessarily separate. There is also a mention of some of the criteria that might be used for judging the chosen works.

So, in summary, a good introduction should include the following:

- A clear explanation of any key terms (in the case of the examples given, 'gains from the Revolution' and 'self-interest').
- A clear explanation of why there might be different interpretations.
- Some indication of the direction in which the chosen works are going to go.
- An initial judgement on the question.

My progress

Using the examples on pages 46–48, write an effective introduction to your own question and then indicate why you think it will work for you.

My introduction

This will help me because …

_____

_____

_____

_____

4.6 Avoiding narrative and description

It is important to remain analytical and evaluative throughout your answer. Answers that are largely descriptive – of both the chosen works and the events being discussed – will not gain the best marks. This is not to say that narrative or descriptive history is necessarily bad history, rather it is not rewarded in the mark scheme that will be used to assess your work. The golden rule to remember is that it must have an *argument*.

The plan you have drawn up should help to stop you simply telling the story, but it is important that you are clear as to what is meant by narrative and description before you start writing. You should already be aware of the need to remain focused and analytical from your examined units, where the emphasis of essays is on making a judgement or asserting different views of an issue.

Look at the following two paragraphs written in answer to the question '**What is your view on the extent to which the Holocaust was the result of a long-term plan by the Nazis?**'

Which of the two paragraphs answers the question and which simply tells you what happened?

Paragraph A

The outbreak of the war changed the situation for the Jews in Europe. Until the outbreak of the war there were only a few hundred thousand Jews under Nazi control in Germany, Austria and Bohemia. The conquest of Poland in 1939 added another three million. Then, in June 1941, following the invasion of Russia, three million more came under Nazi control. SS *Einsatzgruppen* followed the invading army and rounded up large numbers of Jews. They carried out mass shootings, murdering some seven hundred thousand Jews between 1941 and 1942. As Farmer states, 'this was only the start of the buildup'. From September 1941, Jews were forced to wear the yellow Star of David, so that they could be easily identified.

Paragraph B

Martin Broszat suggests that the invasion of Russia was a turning point in Nazi policy towards the Jews because it realigned Nazi objectives. Instead of considering a policy of resettlement, initially in the French colony of Madagascar, then in camps and ghettos in occupied Poland, the war became an ideological conflict directed at the extermination of 'Jewish Bolshevism'. By the Spring of 1942 over a million Russian Jews had been murdered. There is little doubt that these massacres signified an escalation in Nazi policy towards the Jews and prepared the way for the Holocaust. It was only the realisation that the war against Russia would not be won quickly that systematic extermination began. The main priorities of the regime changed from resettlement to supplying the army with men and equipment. Resettlement would have been a practical problem and, in these circumstances, Broszat is right to argue that the introduction of the Holocaust 'was a "way out" of a blind alley into which the National Socialists had maneuvered themselves'.

Paragraph B maintains much more focus on answering the question, whereas Paragraph A is a descriptive account of the escalation of the Holocaust.

How do you avoid simply telling the story? One of the best ways is to ensure that the opening sentence of each paragraph relates back to the question. This will also help to keep you focused on the actual issues in the question and should prevent you from writing narrative.

Opening sentences

⒜

Read the following possible opening sentences for the question **'What is your view about how successful Mussolini's economic policies were?'**

1 Mussolini inherited a large budget deficit and a total of half a million unemployed.
2 As Hibbert points out, De Stefani abolished price-fixing and rent controls and reduced government expenditure.
3 The move towards protection resulted in economic problems before the start of the Wall Street Crash.
4 **Autarky** had some impressive successes.
5 According to Denis Mack Smith, the 'battle for grain' was only superficially successful.
6 In 1870 grain production had been 40 million quintals and reached 60 million by 1930 and 80 million by 1939.
7 The 'battle for land' was marked by notable successes.
8 The most famous land reclamation scheme was the draining of the Pontine Marshes near Rome.
9 Duggan's view is that the least successful of the 'battles' was the 'the battle for births'.
10 The balance sheet of the policy of autarky was not altogether negative.

Highlight in green the sentences that introduce an idea that directly answers the question.

Highlight in red the sentences that simply describe what happened to the economy during Mussolini's time in power.

My progress

Having completed the activity above, now apply this to your own title.
Title of my Investigation:

_____

_____

What issues are you going to discuss? These have been identified in your plan and your reading of the chosen works.
Construct at least one opening sentence for each of the key points your Investigation will discuss. Ensure that the sentence introduces an idea relevant to the actual question and does not simply describe facts. Remember each point should be linked to the chosen works.

1 _____

2 _____

3 _____

4 _____

5 _____

6 _____

4.7 Discussion rather than explanation

You should have already noted that you must answer the question you have set. That may seem obvious, but just simply explaining a list of reasons and describing the views in the chosen works will not score high marks. There is a big difference between explaining a range of issues from interpretations and weighing up the importance of those ideas and issues in relation to valid criteria. You will also have to ensure that this assessment goes on throughout the essay if you want to reach the highest levels in the mark scheme.

This means that you will not only need to introduce your argument in the opening sentence of each paragraph, but that you will need to develop the argument during the paragraph before reaching a supported judgement about the issue you have been discussing. In developing your argument you will need to consider both sides of the argument. What evidence is there to support or challenge the argument, whether or not it is found in a chosen work? You may discuss supplementary reading to support or challenge your argument. Why is one argument more compelling than the other? That last point will be your judgement.

Read the following example paragraph which is part of an answer to the question '**What is your view about the reasons for the outbreak of the Second World War in Europe in 1939?**'

An important factor in the outbreak of the Second World War was the Nazi-Soviet Pact signed on 24 August 1939, which Shore argues is 'one of the most significant diplomatic events in the twentieth century'. This agreement between Germany and Russia stated that the two countries would attack and divide Poland between them and would not go to war with each other. The agreement with Russia meant that Germany was then free to attack in the west and need not fear a war on two fronts as had happened in 1914. As a result of the treaty Germany would gain half of Poland, which would strengthen it territorially. It also meant that Britain and France, who had signed a treaty to protect Poland, would have to come to its defence and this would lead to a European War. Hitler hoped that because they would not have the support of Russia, Britain and France would not take such action and that he would be free to fight a local war and therefore he invaded Poland on 1 September 1939. Britain and France however did support Poland and declared war on Germany on 3 September, starting a general European war. Shore gives significant weight to the role of the Pact, primarily as a result of his own research, which focused on the relationships between high-ranking diplomats in Europe in the late 1930s.

The paragraph is not entirely successful.

- It explains the role that the Nazi-Soviet Pact and Hitler's subsequent invasion of Poland played in the outbreak of the war, but it does not discuss the importance of the Pact as a factor in the outbreak of the war in Europe.
- How important was the Pact? Did it have an impact on the type of war that broke out?
- It begins to explore the validity of Shore's argument towards the end, but this is not developed very far.

Producing the right kind of paragraphs

Read the following paragraph in response to the same question: **'What is your view about the reasons for the outbreak of the Second World War in Europe in 1939?'**

One of the major ways of determining the reasons for the war is in understanding how Hitler was able to gain the diplomatic confidence to attack Poland. According to Shore, the signing of the Nazi-Soviet Non-aggression Pact was the most important reason for this. Its short-term significance in starting the war is seen most clearly in that the Pact was signed only on 24 August and just over a week later Britain and France had declared war against Germany. Shore argues that the war would only start once Hitler had gained sufficient confidence to attack his neighbours, and the Pact was crucial in the timing of Hitler's invasion of Poland, which is what led to the outbreak of war, as it meant that Hitler was no longer faced with the possibility of a war on two fronts. He was determined to avoid the same problems that had befallen Imperial Germany in 1914 and therefore once he had secured Russian non-aggression this gave him the confidence to attack Poland. Therefore, although he had been planning the attack on Poland for some time, certainly since the annexation of Czechoslovakia in March 1939, it was only with the certainty that Russia would not join Britain and France that he was willing to go to war, even if he did not expect Britain and France to aid Poland and start a major conflagration.

Compare this paragraph with the one on page 52 in answer to the same question. This response would reach a higher level than the paragraph on the opposite page.

1   Using a coloured pen highlight what information there is in this paragraph that is not in the response on page 52.

2   This paragraph uses criteria to explore the strength of the Nazi-Soviet Pact argument. Using a different coloured pen highlight where this is done.

3   What is better about the paragraph on this page than the one on page 52?

4   The paragraph on this page starts to discuss the relative importance of the Nazi-Soviet Pact in bringing about the Second World War in Europe. This is done through the use of evaluative words. Make a list of the evaluative words and phrases that are used in the paragraph to argue that the Pact was important.

_____

_____

_____

_____

_____

_____

_____

_____

_____

_____

_____

4.8 Maintaining focus

One of the main demands of the coursework is that you remain focused on the question. Once you start to lose focus you will find yourself slipping down the levels in the mark scheme. It is therefore vitally important that you are always checking that you are answering your question.

Consider the following question:

> What is your view about the extent to which the Nazi regime was largely successful in its policies towards women before 1939?

A good answer might establish the Nazi regime's aims towards women in this period and would establish criteria by which this success can be judged. It should consider whether these aims were achieved through an assessment of the relevant chosen works. Read the following paragraph written in answer to this question.

The Nazis introduced a considerable number of policies aimed specifically at women. The first of these policies was brought in during June 1933 when women were offered interest-free loans if they married and gave up work. The drive to encourage women to leave work continued with Labour Exchanges encouraged to discriminate in favour of men when they were looking for work rather than giving jobs to women. One policy that Stephenson states contributed to the 'erosion of girls' education and promotion of indoctrination' was the limiting of educational opportunities for girls, as in January 1934 the number who were allowed to enter higher education was limited and this was further reduced in 1937. Meanwhile, grammar school education for girls was abolished and they were banned from studying Latin which was a requirement for university and this restriction therefore prevented them from applying.

Such a paragraph would not achieve a high mark as it is not focused on the success of Nazi policies towards women. Instead it simply describes some of the policies that the Nazis implemented and only uses a chosen work to aid description.

Ways an answer can lose focus

There are a number of ways in which an answer can lose focus:

- It can be descriptive of policy or events rather than analytical.
- It can be descriptive of chosen works without being critical of them.
- The material in the paragraph may be relevant to the topic but not the question.

Another way in which an answer can lose focus is to answer a different question. Consider the following question and sample paragraph beneath it:

> What is your view about the extent to which the Soviet Union was to blame for the outbreak of the Cold War by 1949?

McCauley argues that the Cold War was caused by ideological differences that can be traced back to the Russian Revolution of 1917. The western powers were fearful of communism spreading to other nations, particularly with the Soviet view of 'world revolution'. However, the Soviet Union felt threatened as it was the only communist country and was surrounded by capitalist states. The Soviet Union and western powers also had different views of the ways in which the economy should be run, with the West supporting capitalism and the Soviet Union wanting it to be under state control. These differing ideologies inevitably led to conflict once the common enemy of Germany had been defeated in 1945.

In this instance the answer focused on the causes of the Cold War and did not consider who was to blame.

Eliminating irrelevance

Perhaps one of the most difficult things to do is to ensure that the whole paragraph remains focused on the question and that there are no sentences or sections of a paragraph that are not relevant.

Consider the following question and then read the paragraph below in answer to it.

What is your view about how important Britain's control of the seas was in the struggle against Napoleon?

Knight argues that Napoleon never saw the importance of sea power and suffered as a result. His genius was in land warfare and here rapid movement and concentration of force was the key. He attempted this at Trafalgar but the joint Franco-Spanish fleet were defeated by Nelson. ~~Napoleon could not invade Britain but he had already given up this idea and marched his invasion force from Boulogne to the Danube where he defeated Austria. Britain's coalitions could not withstand Napoleon's forces.~~ However, the supremacy of the navy allowed them to control the seas and blockade France, hitting French trade and war supplies. It also meant that Britain could supply and reinforce its forces in the key war in Portugal and Spain, which drained many French resources. ~~This war had begun as a result of Napoleon's desire for even more European expansion. The Spanish resisted and Napoleon was drawn into a long conflict – the 'Spanish ulcer'. This did not deter him from embarking on another war against Austria in 1809.~~

The crossed-out sections have no real relevance to the issue being discussed in the paragraph and would be seen as a 'loss of focus'.

Now consider the following question and the answer paragraph and highlight or draw a line through the information that is irrelevant, then explain your deletions by writing comments around the paragraph.

What is your view about the reasons for Cromwell's fall from power in 1540?

Cromwell's fall from power in 1540 was the result of many factors. He had served Henry well, had been the architect behind the measures that resulted in the break with Rome and had secured the Royal Supremacy, but this was similar to Cardinal Wolsey who achieved a great deal for Henry. Cromwell had probably achieved more for the King than any other royal servant, bringing about what has been described as revolution in government and making Henry wealthy through the Dissolution of the Monasteries. Despite numerous achievements, he had alienated many among the nobility because of his background. His position was further weakened by factional struggles between the religious reformists, which Cromwell represented, and the more Catholic faction under Norfolk and Gardiner, which emerged triumphant following the disastrous Cleves marriage, which Cromwell had been responsible for organising. Howard was able to use his attractive niece, Catherine Howard, to woo Henry and persuade him to believe stories he was told about his Chief Minister.

My progress

Ensure that you check all of your paragraphs to ensure that they are answering the actual question set. You should do this as you write each paragraph. Go back to your question and ask yourself in what ways is this answering the question and are there any parts that are not directly answering it. Delete those parts that are not directly relevant.

4.9 Integrating supplementary reading

One of the best ways to show your skills in evaluating interpretations is to test the arguments of your chosen works by using the evidence from your supplementary reading. It sounds complicated, but it need not be – it just requires some thought. Let's have a look at an example on Anglo-Saxon England where this has been done.

> What is your view about how great the influence of the Godwin family was in causing tension during Edward the Confessor's reign?

Edward the Confessor was the Anglo-Saxon king who died in 1066. There was a powerful noble family, the Godwins, in his kingdom and historians have debated about how far they undermined his authority and created problems for him. Hill's* view is that the Godwins were determined to disrupt Edward's reign and the revolt of 1051 aimed, more than anything, to ensure Edward changed his choice of advisers.

This section is directly focused on the question and discusses a key point about the Godwins' influence. The issue is whether they tried to influence the succession.

The historian Campbell contrasts somewhat with Hill, and claims that there was a revolt in 1051 by the Godwins with the aim of 'changing the king's plans for the succession'. This plan was to make William of Normandy his heir. This would have indicated a considerable amount of influence. However, this view can be challenged. According to Brown, there is no evidence that William of Normandy visited England until after the Godwin family had been exiled and the source for the visit, Florence of Worcester, merely says that William came and was 'entertained honourably'. There is no record of his being made the heir. Campbell and Hill rely on Norman sources such as William of Poitiers and William of Jumieges who assert that Edward loved William as a brother or a son. Therefore, the historians who make too much use of them may be overstating the commitment of Edward to making William his heir and hence the importance of the Godwins in seemingly undermining this.

The chosen work, Hill, is evaluated through a consideration of the findings of other historians.

Of course, the evaluation could be taken further, but this is an example of how supplementary reading can be integrated.

*Chosen work

Using supplementary reading

Look at the sample paragraph in answer to the question '**What is your view about how far Hitler can be seen as a 'weak dictator' in the years 1933–45?**'

David Lloyd George visited Germany in 1936 and said to his daughter 'Certainly Heil Hitler! I say so because he is a great man'. Though this was three years after he came to power and he had not yet taken over large parts of Europe. Many intentionalists think that his determination in foreign policy made him a great leader. For example, Alan Bullock, Wilfred Knapp and John Lukacs all think that his greatest moves were in his foreign policy. As they agree, this means he was a strong leader.

The evidence concerns Hitler as a 'great man' and has limited links with the debate about the way he ruled as a dictator. The three historians are linked by being 'intentionalists' but this isn't explained. The argument is not very strong in relation to the question.

There is little to evaluate the views of the historians and whether they all agree does not make them right or wrong.

1   How could the material be linked more directly to the idea of 'weak dictator'?

_____

_____

2   What does the answer need to do to explain and assess the historians' views more?

_____

_____

My progress

Write a paragraph on your own chosen title which evaluates a chosen work with evidence from supplementary reading. Check how well you have done by filling in the list below.

1   What is the view in the chosen work?

_____

_____

2   How is it evaluated?

_____

_____

3   What is the supplementary reading and how does it support or challenge the work?

_____

_____

4   What shows you are linking all this to your actual question?

_____

_____

4.10 Evaluation of interpretations

If you look up the word 'evaluate' in the glossary at the back of this workbook you will see that it refers to giving value to the interpretations that you have discussed. This means that instead of simply providing a list of reasons as to why, for example, the American Revolution occurred, you would weigh up the persuasiveness of the views found in the chosen works in causing the American Revolution, by assessing these against a criterion.

Learning how to evaluate or explain how persuasive a particular interpretation or argument is in explaining an event is not an easy skill to master. As a student of History, you may easily slip into the pattern of simply listing events, for example learning six reasons why Hitler came to power. But you should have discovered that this will not get you very high up the mark scheme.

Let's consider how you might approach evaluating the factors and arguments for the following essay:

> What is your view about the extent to which Hitler's personal popularity explains why the Nazis gained support in the period from 1929 to 1933?

You might find this easier to do as a chart. An example has been done at the bottom of this page. The arguments in the left column should stem from your chosen works.

If you just used the information in the second column you would explain the reasons why Hitler came to power, but the arguments in the third column give a value or evaluate the importance of those factors in increasing Nazi support. The first reason is decided as the most persuasive because a direct link can be found to support in the elections.

You might find it even more helpful to add another column in which you give each factor a mark out of six depending on its importance in increasing Nazi support, giving 1 to the most important down to 6 to the least. Such an exercise will force you to make a decision about the importance of factors.

However, you must also remember that you need to be able to support your decision. It is no good simply saying it is the most important reason as that is just **assertion**; you need to explain **why** it is the most important and that is where the information in the third column is vital, and should ideally include the criteria you are using when deciding on an order of importance. Anyone could put numbers from 1 to 6 in a final column, it is your knowledge and understanding of the factors that will allow you to justify your ranking of the factors.

Factor/Argument	Explanation of role	Evaluation of importance
1 Rise in unemployment	Growth in Nazi support after Wall Street Crash, not done well before, offered solutions and appeal to those who had lost jobs	Most important because it was only after the growth in unemployment following WSC that support in elections grew
2 Failure of Weimar	Government's inability to agree on policies meant they looked weak so people turned to other parties	Weimar's inability to deal with unemployment encouraged people to look for an alternative party and they turned to Nazis, therefore quite important
3 Popularity of Hitler	Hitler appealed to many with his oratory, but was also portrayed as a superman who could solve problems, compared with weakness of Weimar	Hitler was able to play on fears of unemployed in his oratory, weakness of Weimar and fear of communism so quite important, but without unemployment and weakness he would not have appealed
4 Reorganisation of Nazi party	Party was reorganised during 1923–24, local leaders were well trained and able to take advantage of situation	The reorganisation allowed them to take advantage of factors 1 and 2
5 Fear of communism	People did not want similar events to Russia so turned to Nazis rather than communists when looking for an alternative	They could have taken advantage of factors 1 and 2 and appealed to unemployed but Hitler's leadership was better and people feared communism regardless after events
6 Propaganda	Able to exploit the situation and portray Hitler as saviour	Used to exploit factors 1, 2, 3, and 5 but without other factors would have been little use as seen before 1929

My progress

Now complete a chart for your own question which evaluates the importance of the interpretations you will consider.

My coursework essay question:

_____

_____

Argument from chosen work	Explanation	Evaluation	Rank	Justification

4.11 Judgement

It is helpful to make interim judgements (summing up at the end of your discussion of each interpretation) as you write your essay, which should lead you to make an overall judgement based on the critical use of evidence. This is part of good essay technique and should also help you when writing the essay answers in all of your examined units. The question you have chosen should lead you to making a judgement about your own view on the question.

You have not asked, for instance, 'Describe the Battle of Hastings' because that does not involve the higher level skill of making a judgement. You have not asked 'Explain why William the Conqueror won the Battle of Hastings' as that could just be an explanation, not a judgement. You might have asked 'What is your view of the reasons why William of Normandy won the Battle of Hastings?' and this would encourage you to assess which reason or reasons were the most important and therefore which chosen work is the most credible. Or you might have asked 'What is your view about how far the Norman victory at Hastings was the result of the leadership of William I?' This involves a clear judgement about the persuasiveness of different interpretations.

So in the course of the essay, it is a good idea to summarise the conclusions to be drawn from each section. Thus, you might look at an explanation in one work that it was not William's skill but rather the weakness of Harold's forces after a long march from Yorkshire. You need to reach a judgement on how persuasive this argument is. Here are some examples:

During the battle of Hastings on 14 October 1066 the Saxon forces formed a powerful shield wall on higher ground. The Normans attacked but could not break the line, but seeing the Normans give way, Huscroft accepts that the Saxons broke ranks and pursued them leaving themselves vulnerable to counter attack.

Thus, though the evidence shows that Harold's men were likely to have been exhausted by their previous fighting and their long march and this may have been a factor, it does not fully explain the outcome. The Saxon forces maintained their battle line effectively against Norman attacks and were confident enough to try to make the victory decisive by pursuing the Normans not once, but twice. This does not suggest over-weary troops

but, if anything, an excess of enthusiasm and vigour which was misapplied – Huscroft does acknowledge that both sides were evenly matched. It was William's ability to take advantage of this that was more important.

This single interpretation cannot be a total explanation, but this judgement would certainly help towards a strong overall conclusion when you come to review all your judgements later.

Now compare this answer with the sample below on the French Revolution.

> What is your view about how far Napoleon destroyed the democratic gains of the French Revolution?

Napoleon Bonaparte was a successful general who took over France in 1799, ending the rule of the Directory government which had governed from 1795. That government had purged the parliament of its enemies on several occasions. Napoleon introduced plebiscites (referenda) to ask the electorate its opinion of issues, but the results were manipulated.

In terms of politics Napoleon could be seen as destroying democracy and meaningful universal male suffrage. All men over 21 could vote but they had to vote for candidates approved by the state. It could be said though that Napoleon did at least keep elements of the Constitution and did not make himself dictator. Sutherland, using the evidence of the rigged plebiscites, sees him introducing dictatorship, but Jordan questions whether it was in fact Napoleon who destroyed democracy because of the Coup of Fructidor under the Directory which together with other purges undermined meaningful democracy. However, Napoleon himself said 'the constitution means nothing to me', though this might not be typical of his views as he tried to introduce a more liberal constitution in 1815.

There is some good material here, but it really needs a judgement. What does this really show? Where is the balance? What is the final conclusion going to be? What does the writer think after looking at this evidence?

Interim judgements

Look again at the paragraph on Napoleon on page 60. Which of these interim judgements do you think might be made on the basis of the evidence in the paragraph?

1

Thus, Napoleon definitely destroyed the gains of the Revolution in terms of democracy and constitutional government.

Is this valid? Explain your answer

_____

_____

_____

2

Napoleon did not destroy the gains of the Revolution because he consulted the people in plebiscities and had universal male suffrage.

Is this valid? Explain your answer

_____

_____

_____

3

Napoleon did not completely destroy the gains of the Revolution in the sense that there was still a constitution and the gains had already been undermined by the previous revolutionary regime. However, he undermined any real hopes for a democratic and constitutional rule by restricting the candidates to be voted for and by rigging plebiscites so though he kept a pretence of democracy it was toothless and without substance.

Is this valid? Explain your answer

_____

_____

_____

My progress

Take a section of your essay and write a clear interim judgement. It should have a clear view of the issue in the question and can relate to the chosen works.

_____

4.12 Example coursework paragraphs

Here are some examples of paragraphs from answers. They should contain evaluation of evidence within an overall argument. There is a commentary on each one.

1 What is your view about the role of Harold in bringing about Norman victory at Hastings in 1066?

Huscroft argues that William succeeded because of the lack of English troops and William's leadership on the battlefield. Golding doesn't say what he thinks is the key reason for the outcome but he thinks that William's army was born of a practical necessity and supports Huscroft's view that William and his army were the most important reasons. However, these views don't take into account Harold's actions. Walker on the other hand thinks that Harold was beaten 'by a better man'; and Hill quotes Stenton, saying 'he lost the battle because his men were unequal to the stress'. Hill is more convincing because he looks at the situation before the battle. Therefore it is clear that Harold was the most important factor.

Chosen works are considered here but they are not well analysed in terms of the explanations they offer. Because Golding agrees with Huscroft does not make their view correct and in any case the basis of it is not explained. There is virtually no evaluation except for the statement that the views don't take into account Harold's actions, but this is not explained. A lot of work seems to be behind this, but it needs to step back and look more carefully at the evidence.

2 What is your view about the extent to which Harold Wilson's economic policies in the period 1964–70 were successful?

Wilson's economic policy can be evaluated by looking at economic growth. O'Hara points to Wilson's goal of increasing growth from around 2.1 per cent a year to 4 per cent a year. In the early part of his government the growth rate accelerated to 2.6 per cent a year. However, by 1970 the economy was growing at 2.1 per cent a year, the same rate as the early 1960s. From this point of view O'Hara argues that Wilson's policy was a failure.

The view that Wilson's policy was a failure because it did not improve economic growth is challenged by Woodward and Tomlinson. Woodward argues that in the context of the period 1856 to 1973 the growth achieved under Wilson was high. By achieving 2.7 per cent growth a year between 1964 and 1968, the economy grew faster than at any other time since the Industrial Revolution. Tomlinson looks at the period 1970 to 2010, arguing that average economic growth slowed in the 1970s and continued at a slower rate than it did under Wilson. Tomlinson also argues that big recessions under Heath in the 1970s, under Thatcher in the 1980s and under Major in the 1990s meant that average economic growth in decades after 1970 was much lower than growth was under Wilson. Therefore, while O'Hara is right to argue that Wilson failed to achieve his own goal of 4 per cent growth, this promoted a period of almost unprecedented economic growth and does not mean that Wilson's economic policy itself was a failure, because in the context of the British economy from 1856 to 2010 Wilson's period was fast growing, implying that he was more successful at economic management than pre-war and other post-war governments. Overall, O'Hara's argument that Wilson was a failure is credible only because he defines success so narrowly, whereas when Wilson's achievements are viewed in the context of a broader sweep of history they seem much more successful.

A clear criterion for judgement is presented here to assess Wilson's success: how successful economic growth was. O'Hara's view is presented and criticised with evidence from other historians. When assessing the validity of O'Hara's argument, the writer ultimately concludes that when measured against the criterion of longer-term growth, Wilson's achievements are successful.

My progress

Here is a checklist to help evaluate the quality of your paragraphs.

- Does the paragraph focus on key arguments in the debate?
- Is there a focus on one or more of the chosen works?
- Is the view of the chosen works made clear?
- Are there any judgements made about the evidence?
- Is the judgement based on any valid criteria or simply asserted?
- Is the paragraph relevant to the title?
- Is there an interim judgement based on the discussion?

Write a paragraph from your essay that deals with one or more chosen works and then complete the checklist.

Does the paragraph focus on key arguments in the debate?

_____

_____

Is there a focus on one or more of the chosen works?

_____

_____

Is the view of the chosen works made clear? Give one example.

_____

_____

Are there any judgements made about the evidence? Give one example.

_____

_____

Is the judgement based on criteria or simply asserted? Give one example.

_____

_____

Is the paragraph relevant to the title? How can you be sure?

_____

_____

Is there an interim judgement based on the discussion? What shows this?

_____

_____

4.13 Writing a conclusion

The **conclusion** should be based on the interim **judgements** made throughout the essay if it is going to be convincing. If all the evidence points to, say, a chosen work that argues that Hitler was a weak dictator because of the poor organisation of Nazi government and his own idle work habits, then that should be the basis of the conclusion.

There is an old-fashioned idea that you need to produce something different and exciting in the conclusion to avoid your essay being 'boring'. This is not true. A conclusion that suddenly reverses all the **arguments** made in the bulk of the essay simply seems jarring to the reader and suggests that you have been ignoring key counter arguments. If you have proposed a clear line of argument at the start, the conclusion should confirm that even if there may be more modifications and qualifications.

In general, the conclusion needs to establish the following:

- A reiteration of the key lines of argument in the chosen works.
- An assessment of the strength of the arguments in the chosen works.
- A final judgement on the question itself, taking into account the findings from the chosen works and supplementary reading.

This conclusion to the question '**What is your view about the extent to which Harold Wilson's economic policies in the period 1964–70 were successful?**' is a good example of a clear but balanced view.

In conclusion, the view that Wilson's economic policy was successful is broadly convincing. O'Hara raises some valid points about specific failures of policy. However, O'Hara mixes up political and economic failures when he makes his argument about devaluation. Also, O'Hara's **criteria** for making a judgement are often quite narrow, Wilson's objectives are not the only criterion for judging the success of his policies, nor is the overall consistency of Wilson's macroeconomic policy. Generally, Wilson's policies led to a good level of growth, judged against Britain's historic economic performance as well as record productivity. Woodward, who considers Wilson's achievements by comparing them to the long-term factors of the British economy, argues that this was 'the most successful period Britain's economy was ever to enjoy'. Additionally, Wilson's setbacks did not stop him from carrying on with his long-term goals. The collapse of the National Plan and the DEA did not stop Wilson from trying to modernise the economy. In fact, as Tomlinson shows, the collapse of the DEA led to a bigger role for the more effective MiniTech, which made Britain's nationalised industries more efficient. Finally, Tomlinson is right to argue that, judged on Wilson's socialist values, and judged against later governments, the economy was also generally successful. Wilson's economy saw high levels of employment and growing equality.

Dissecting a conclusion

Look again at the conclusion on page 64. Identify the answer it gives to the question in no more than two sentences.

_____

_____

Now look at the example conclusion below to the question '**What is your view about how far religion determined the taking of sides in the English Civil War?**'

Despite Gentles' unique focus on the religion of ordinary soldiers rather than the gentry, and Morrill's examination of a range of different counties, it can be argued that Wood's argument that self-interest was the determining factor is the strongest. He has considered only one county, allowing him to explore the issue in a level of depth that Gentles, in focusing on the whole country, and Morrill, in looking at as many different counties as possible, have been unable to do. The majority of historians only examine the reasons behind the gentry class taking sides, however Wood has looked past them to a previously neglected lower class group, and has evaluated existing literature on Derbyshire to inform his judgement, something not done by either Gentles or Morrill. Wood's view is the most convincing because, in concluding that self-interest was important, his findings are in line with much of the evidence found elsewhere, such as Dore's findings that local quarrels and selfishness led to individuals of all classes taking sides. Therefore, economic factors and self-interest – not religion – were the most important influences for choosing sides in the English Civil War.

Can you identify the answer to the question?

_____

_____

My progress

Write a possible conclusion to your question – it doesn't matter if you haven't finished the research. Just try to form an opinion on what you've done so far.

```

```

Which example is it more like – the one on page 64 or the one in the activity above? Why?

_____

_____

_____

_____

Self-assessment

As this coursework is an independent essay, the amount of help your teacher can give is limited by the rules set down by the body that regulates all A level examinations. This means that your teacher cannot offer detailed comments and can only look at one draft, and then cannot make specific suggestions. Your work is going to be marked against set guidelines, so it is important that you try to apply the mark scheme yourself before you hand in the work in its final form for marking.

If you get used to making use of the mark scheme as you're writing, then this should help you to be sure that you are on the right lines.

Looking at your essay, you have to ask yourself whether it meets the requirements. You can do this by filling out the tables below and completing the questions on these pages. Don't wait to the end to fill this in. Once you start writing, refer to it as much as possible.

Key questions to ask	Yes/mostly/partly/no	What do I need to do to meet it?
Have I related everything in my essay to the question?		
Have I included a lot of description rather than explaining and assessing?		
Have I included interim judgements?		
Have I made an overall judgement at the end?		
Have I used detailed knowledge?		
Have I fully assessed the three chosen works?		
Have I explored the differences between the chosen works?		
Have I explained why the chosen works contain differences?		
Have I reached a reasoned conclusion on which of the chosen works presents the most persuasive argument?		
Have I referenced my reading in footnotes and included them in the bibliography?		

Evaluation of evidence

Evaluation means putting a value on the interpretations. Please select in the table below the ways in which you have evaluated arguments in your essay.

I have evaluated the chosen works by:

	Chosen work 1 Name:	Chosen work 2 Name:	Chosen work 3 Name:
Corroborating (backing up) with evidence from supplementary reading			
Criticising with evidence from supplementary reading			
Considering what evidence they have used			
Considering the research focus of the historians			
Comparing the chosen work to the others			
Explaining the differences between this work and the others			
Explaining why there are differences between this work and the others			

One way you can check your evaluation of interpretations is to highlight evaluative words in your essay. Check how many of the following evaluative words and phrases appear in your work.

This interpretation:
- is/is not persuasive
- is/is not typical
- is/is not complete
- neglects to take into account …
- overestimates …
- puts too much emphasis on …
- however, (Taylor argues …, however, this …)
- is too influenced
- is/is not supported by
- is/is not corroborated by

Footnotes and bibliography

In carrying out your research you will have seen that many of the books and articles that you have used contain footnotes at the bottom of the page, or endnotes at the end of each chapter, in which the author acknowledges other works from which he or she obtained their information and do not try to claim that it is their own research.

Similarly, at the end of the book there will be a bibliography. This is somewhat different from footnotes or endnotes. A bibliography is a list of all the books that an author has referred to during their research, even if they have not quoted from them or taken ideas and information from them.

Both of these should appear in your piece of coursework. There are a number of reasons for this:

- You need to show where you obtained the knowledge, sources and Interpretations that you are using.
- You cannot claim that ideas and knowledge are your own when they have been taken from other people's work. That would be plagiarism.
- It is an academic convention and this is an academic piece of work.
- It is good practice for the future as higher education institutions will expect it; even reports for businesses contain them.

Bibliography

Although the bibliography appears at the end of your essay it might be a good idea to add to it as you write your essay. This means that you need to keep a record of your reading as you go along. Even if you could, it would be very time consuming to have to go back to find out all the titles, authors and other details that are needed to put together a bibliography.

What should the bibliography contain and how should it be set out?

The bibliography should be a record of all the works you have referred to when doing your research, including chosen works and supplementary reading. You should clearly differentiate between your chosen works and other readings in the bibliography.

Although not essential, these works can be organised into sections with headings:

- Chosen works
- Supplementary works.

There is a variety of different methods for writing a bibliography, and you can use any of them. Generally, however, the works should be ordered alphabetically according to the surname of the author, and will contain the author's name, the title of the book, the publisher and the date of publication, for example:

Pope, R., *War and Society in Britain*, Longman, London, 1991

In terms of books with more than one author then the following format should be used:

Dicken, M. and Fellows, N., *Britain 1603–1760*, Hodder, London, 2015

When there is an editor:

Boyce, D. and O'Day, A. (eds.) *Parnell in Perspective*, Routledge, London, 1991

With articles from journals:

Goodlad, G., Feb 2013, 'Margaret Thatcher and the Soviet Union', *Twentieth Century History Review*, vol. 8., no 3, pages 26–29

With other materials, such as web pages, the format is again different. The most basic entry for a website consists of the author name(s), page title, website title, sponsoring institution/publisher, date published, medium and date accessed.

You may discover that different institutions require different formats, but the main thing with this essay is to be consistent.

Footnotes

All the works that appear in the footnotes should appear in the bibliography, however the format will be different.

Footnotes acknowledge where you have used information from another source and show that you are not claiming it to be your own. As a general rule, make sure that you reference every idea that is not your own. Facts that are indisputable and are widely written about (e.g. the Second World War started in 1939) do not need to be referenced.

Most word processing software makes it very easy to insert a number in the text and the reference at the bottom of the page (or at the end of the work if you are using endnotes). Once again there is a wide range of different styles, but it would make sense if they were in a similar format to the bibliography.

The main difference between footnotes and the bibliography is that the footnote will include the page or pages from which you have drawn your information. For example:

Rex Pope, *War and Society in Britain*, (Longman, London, 1991) pages 48–49.

If you use the same book or article consecutively then you may simply put:

ibid page 50.

Similarly, if the same book is used later in your essay you do not need to write out the full details but can simply put the name of the author and the page used.

Your school may have a policy on the system they want you to use and it would be worth checking to see before following the guidance given here. The exam board has no set requirement for the system that is used, but consistency is the key.

Research skills and plagiarism

Plagiarism is pretending that someone else's work is your own. It is unlikely that students will get someone else to write their coursework, especially as the skills involved are unique to this particular course. However, a great deal of material is available on websites and can be copied and pasted easily. Textbooks, articles and specialist studies can be photocopied or photographed.

Many students like to build up a body of material like this, but it is very important when researching to ensure that there is a distinction between work read, consulted, used and made part of their own work, and material that is inserted without any acknowledgement.

That sort of plagiarism is not as obvious as the use of someone else's whole work but it is just as important to avoid it.

The use of books and articles

When research is undertaken it is vital for notes to be made that get to the heart of ideas, arguments and supporting factual information. If a particular argument is used then it is often helpful to quote briefly, but long extracts should be avoided and essays should not consist of a series of quotations. When a direct quote is made then this should be footnoted with the page reference in the book. If an idea is taken from a history book then it should also be acknowledged. It would obviously not be appropriate to acknowledge where you obtained every fact. If you are starting without previous knowledge, let's say of the Battle of Hastings, and you read a history book or article that tells you it was on 14 October 1066 then you would not acknowledge where you got this information as it

is common knowledge. However, if you decide to use a particular argument about the battle's outcome from a book or article then this should be acknowledged.

The use of primary evidence

If you use any primary sources it is necessary to reference the evidence in a footnote to show where the argument came from and to make clear that the interpretation is not yours but is taken from a source.

The use of internet material

This material can often be copied very easily. It is extremely important that sections of work are not completed through unacknowledged lifting from online encyclopaedias or articles. As with books it is strongly recommended that notes are taken from the material and that arguments and ideas are acknowledged. If there is a quotation then the web address and the date you accessed the site should be included.

Books containing historiographical summaries

Many books – both those aimed at A level students and academic history books – outline the historiography of the topic they are dealing with. This is often very helpful in coursework, but students should not give the impression that they have read and used the works mentioned and should acknowledge that they are using an account of different views by an author, not that they have consulted the historians mentioned when they have not. These sorts of summaries should only be used as supplementary works, and not as chosen works.

Read this extract from *Access to History America, Civil War and Westward Expansion* by Alan Farmer (Hodder Education, 2015, pages 108–9). It could be used for the question, '**What is your view about the reasons why there was a Civil War in the USA 1861–5?**'

In the 1920s, 'progressive' historians claimed that clashes between interest groups underpinned events in history, claimed that the war was a contest between plantation agriculture and industrialising capitalism. According to progressives, economic issues (such as the tariff) were what really divided the power-brokers – northern manufacturers and southern planters. The confederacy could thus be seen as fighting for the preservation of a stable, agrarian civilisation in the face of the grasping ambitions of northern businessmen … In the 1940s, revisionist historians denied that sectional conflicts, whether over slavery, state rights or industry versus agriculture were genuinely divisive. The differences between North and South, wrote revisionist historian Avery Craven, were 'no greater than those existing at different times between East and West'. In the revisionist view, far more united than divided the two sections: sectional quarrels could and should have been accommodated peacefully. Far from being irrepressible, the war was brought on by extremists on both sides … Historians have now come full circle. The progressive and revisionist schools are currently dormant. Lincoln's view that slavery was 'somehow' the cause of the war is generally accepted. While the Confederacy might claim its justification to be the protector of state rights, in truth, it was one state right – the right to preserve slavery – that impelled the Confederate states' separation. Slavery defined the South, permeating every aspect.

The extract is a highly useful survey of different ideas. It gives a starting point for the student to find different interpretations and to test them. However, its style is not necessarily the style of an A level student. An essay that is plagiarised might begin like this:

> There are many different reasons for the Civil War. 'Progressive' historians have claimed that clashes between different interest groups caused the war. They have claimed that the war was a contest between plantation owners and industrialising capitalism and war was about issues such as the tariff. However revisionist historians like Avery Craven had argued that differences were 'no greater than those existing at different times between east and west' and the war was brought on by extremists. These views are now dormant. It is generally accepted that Lincoln's view was right and slavery was 'somehow' the cause as slavery permeated every aspect of the South.

However, the false impression is given that the writer has read Craven and the analysis of the historiography, which is Alan Farmer's, is being passed off as the student's own. There are even direct quotations that are not acknowledged. It is fine to get a general idea when you start off the contrasting views but this student has simply taken a short cut.

My progress

Use the following checklist to ensure that you have taken all relevant information from each resource you consider.

Noted title, author, date of publication and publisher?	
Summary of key arguments	
References to other works that can be followed up	
Other research that supports it?	
Other research that contradicts it?	
How far does it meet my criteria for judgement?	

Research logs

You are required to submit a resource record that will act as a log of the reading you have carried out. It is also useful to keep a log of your initial research and ideas. The log below has been filled in to give you an idea of what to do. As you work on your coursework you can fill out the blank version at the back of this workbook.

Getting started – deciding on a topic and making sure your title works

Initial idea for essay	Why I chose it	Initial search for resources
20 July What caused the US Civil War? Was the South to blame? Was it just slavery? Was Lincoln wrong? Or Can slavery in the Southern states before 1861 be justified?	I found this interesting in my A level Paper 2 course but want to know about this in more depth. We did look at some theories but only for a few lessons. There is a lot of material available and different views to look at. Decided against the question on slavery after discussion with teacher as too much like an ethical question.	Did an internet search on the US Civil War and started to look at A level texts. Found an Access to History book with a good section on causes. Found websites on the debate.

Refining the title and interpretations

Draft title	Explanation showing different interpretations	Supplementary reading	Any advice from teacher
20 September What is your view about why the Civil War broke out in the USA in 1861? 20 October What is your view about whether slavery was the main cause of the US Civil War?	Revisionists question importance of deep divisions about slavery and the progressive school think economic factors more important. Changed because the role of slavery gives me a clear starting point.	I found sources online – for example, Southern states own explanation for secession and Lincoln's speeches in 1861.	In a discussion, tutor suggested that 'why' might lead to a list and that I should make sure that my title leads clearly to a discussion. Topic approved but changed to 'What is your view about the extent to which slavery was the main cause of the US Civil War?'

Initial interpretations research

Date	Resource	Key ideas	Evaluation
20 October	Alan Farmer, America: Civil War and Westward Expansion 1803-90 Hodder, 2015	Outlines different theories like Progressives in 1920s arguing for economic issues; Revisionists arguing for just extremists. Book's own view is that slavery was key issue not states' rights because of economic importance.	Need to find more information to justify economic importance of slavery to South to see if view is supported. Question the view – see if slavery really was being threatened or was it just an excuse?

Sample resource record

Centre Number:

Candidate Name:

Resources used The three chosen works for the assignment must be asterisked*	Page/web reference	Student comments	Student date(s) when accessed	Teacher initials and date resource record checked
Alan Farmer, America: Civil War and Westward Expansion 1803-90 Hodder, 2015*	Pages 23-48	Outlines different theories – Progressives in 1920s arguing for economic issues; Revisionists arguing for just extremists. Book's own view is that slavery was key issue not states' rights because of economic importance. Provides a contrasting view to that found in Smith so is appropriate as a chosen work.	20 October	
Richard Nicholson, The American Civil War Penguin, 1992	Pages 10-29	This study looks to states' rights as the most important cause. It is quite broad in its focus and generally emphasises views found in other works from earlier in the 20th century. I decided not to use it as one of my chosen works as it is quite brief and does not consider any new research. I may use it to evaluate the views of other historians.		

Getting started – deciding on a topic and making sure your title works

Initial idea for essay	Why I chose it	Initial search for resources

Refining the title and interpretations

Draft title	Explanation showing different interpretations	Supplementary reading	Any advice from teacher

Initial interpretations research

Date	Resource	Key ideas	Evaluation

Sample resource record

Centre Number:

Candidate Name:

Resources used The three chosen works for the assignment must be asterisked*	Page/web reference	Student comments	Student date(s) when accessed	Teacher initials and date resource record checked

→

Resources used The three chosen works for the assignment must be asterisked*	Page/web reference	Student comments	Student date(s) when accessed	Teacher initials and date resource record checked